Winning Play Sequences
in Modern Football

WINNING
Play Sequences
IN MODERN FOOTBALL

Drew Tallman

Parker Publishing Company, Inc.   West Nyack, N. Y.

© 1971 BY

PARKER PUBLISHING COMPANY, INC.
WEST NYACK, N. Y.

LIBRARY OF CONGRESS
CATALOG CARD NUMBER: 73-134519

PRINTED IN THE UNITED STATES OF AMERICA
ISBN—0-13-961045-6
BC

DEDICATED TO

Jim and Mary Ann McGowan
who have done so much for football and athletics

Kick Off!

This book gives insight into strategies, techniques, ideas, principles and theories in attacking defenses through different sequences of plays. Blocking combinations and patterns are illustrated versus specific defenses, and the football coach can get ideas on attacking defenses in general with the plays of the offensive series listed. Also, through the use of this book, the coach will be better able to defense these sequences of plays.

Series or sequences of plays alone are not the answer to winning football. The overall program—including proper and correct fundamentals, techniques, drills, teaching techniques, organization, winter and spring programs, coaching methods, and psychological ideas—makes or breaks a football team. However, this is the first book written on every series and sequence of plays in modern football. The author believes that, with such an organized presentation of sequences of plays, the football coach can better organize himself when attacking or defending these plays.

The book illustrates, in nuts-and-bolts detail, the winning sequences of plays employed by most teams in one form or another throughout the nation. The series include the Green Bay pro sweep, power series, Split T option, inside belly, outside belly, triple option, quick pitch, cross-buck, sprint-out or roll-out pass, and the drop-back pass. Other various sequence of plays are also illustrated. The strengths and advantages of the sequence of plays, execution desired, personnel needed and formations necessary for the series are fully explained. The major play itself is discussed in complete detail, including the blocking schemes versus all defenses and coaching points of every offensive position. Numerous running plays, passes, bootlegs, screens, and so forth are given to the coach so he can attack defenses in a more systematic manner. The important teaching techniques to exploit the series are presented in detail also.

The ideas, material and information were accumulated through a great deal of research, readings, talks, clinics, films and general observation. What is executed by one school may not be appropriate for another. However, all of the material here has been used successfully at one time or another.

DREW TALLMAN

7

ACKNOWLEDGMENTS

Appreciation is expressed to the many people who assisted and contributed in the preparation of this book.

I am indebted to some great coaches who offered and gave valuable insights into the game of football: Matty Certosimo; Ted Dunn, Springfield College; Chuck Klausing, West Virginia University; and George Paterno, Michigan State University.

And special thanks must go to a beautiful wife, Sue, who spends so much time with football and gives a great deal of support and faith to the boys who play the game.

Table of Contents

9

Winning Play Sequences
in Modern Football

1

A Look at Play Sequences
(Series)

> *To my way of thinking it is a great mistake to try to pick individual plays from the various sound systems of offense and group them together to form an attack. When this is done there is no real sequence of plays and since the true value in any attack is its ability to look the same and still strike at different areas in the defense the sound concept and thorough exploitation of a real system is of vital importance.[1]*
>
> —*Bud Wilkinson*

Series, defined by the dictionary, is a group or a number of related or similar things; arranged, ranged, or occurring in temporal, spatial, or other order or succession; sequence. Sequence is termed as the following of one thing after another; order of succession; something that follows; continuous. Football play sequence or series can, therefore, be defined as a group or a number of related plays arranged or occurring in temporal, spatial or other order of succession.

Building a Series

The following is a list of plays that could be realized in a series—more or less can be employed:

1. *Outside*—One good basic play, usually the best play of the series (for example, the quick pitch play from the quick pitch series). This is considered a wide play.
2. *Off-Tackle*—Since the quick pitch is a wide maneuver, the next play should be off-tackle. This would be a slant off-tackle by another ballcarrier (faking the quick pitch and handing off to the next back).

---

[1] Charles "Bud" Wilkinson, *Oklahoma Split T Football* (New York, New York: Prentice-Hall, Inc., 1952) p. 241.

3. *Middle*—Another play coming within the sequence would consist of faking the quick pitch and handing off to a back coming up the middle (an example would be a quick trap or cross action by the offensive lineman).

4. *Keeper*—This would be the quarterback keeping the ball after one or more fakes from the original basic play. (An example would be faking the quick pitch, faking the slant off-tackle, and having the quarterback keep the ball by running outside.)

5. *Play Action Pass*—This would be a play pass coming off one or more fakes in the backfield. (The quarterback, faking the quick pitch, faking the slant off-tackle, then pulling up and passing the ball to either the quick pitch man going on a flare route or the split end doing some type of *in* maneuver; i.e. curl, slant, drag, post, etc.)

6. *Screen Pass*—The screen would consist of possibly faking one or more plays and throwing a screen pass away from the original play. (An example would be the quarterback faking the quick pitch, faking the slant run, dropping back as if to play action pass the original play, and then screening to another back or end away from the play action side.)

Why Employ Series or Plays?

Plays of an offense are utilized within a series for a number of reasons. An important point is: All plays are listed in a logical, systematic order. They are not haphazardly pulled out of a hat in the hope that the team moves the ball. Plays, therefore, are organized with the intent that they will be easily remembered and understood. Another important reason is, it is easier for the quarterback or coach to call plays. Plays are arranged in groups and the quarterback can associate the plays within the series and easily remember the order in which they are called. Finally, and probably the most important aspect of play sequences, is that, when plays are grouped in similarity, and all come off a certain action in the backfield, it can be very confusing for the defensive team. When the defensive players get habitized to a certain play over and over again, they become accustomed to the running ballcarrier. When the same action is seen in the backfield, the defensive players, in most instances, go where the ball has been handed off before. However, now they find the ball has now been faked and given to another offensive back from the same series. An example would be when the defense is continually confronted with the outside belly and comes hard for the fullback. At a certain point, however, the quarterback pulls the ball out of the fullback and comes out passing the ball on a play action pass. This will be explained later in the chapter.

Attack Defenses According to Coverage

It is important for the offense, with the utilization of its play sequences, to attack defensive alignments according to their coverage. Locate a weakness and attack it. Be able to employ the base play versus all defensive alignments and drill all blocking combinations repeatedly. Certain defensive alignments and adjustments may inhibit one series of play but might enhance another. It is up to the coach to learn, understand, and locate in a game weaknesses that may occur. Once weaknesses are found, the coach must attack, with the proper play sequences, that area of the defense which is most vulnerable.

Personnel Variances

In most cases, personnel will have a great deal to do with the type and kind of series a coach employs. If a coach has a fine quarterback who can pass the ball well, he may want to develop a good drop-back pass series with flankers and split ends. If he has a fine tailback, he may want to scrap the belly series and utilize more of a good running attack from a tailback formation.

Personnel makes or breaks a team over an entire season. It is up to the coach to utilize his personnel to the best possible advantage. Certain series are beneficial with different ballplayers. When personnel are placed in their proper positions, the series may go with greater ease and efficiency.

Proper Blocking Combination for a Successful Series

For a series to work successfully versus opponents, it must utilize proper strategical blocking combination. On numerous occasions it is the blocking at the line of scrimmage that makes a play or series execute successfully.

There are many coaches who utilize simple blocking rules within their offensive system to make it easy for the players to learn. While this is good and necessary, there are instances when better blocking combinations can be employed at the line of scrimmage. The coach should find, study, and understand the best and most efficient methods in blocking certain play sequences. The plays for each series will improve and more success will result. When doing this it is best for the coach to set up a standard of good solid blocking rules that apply to a particular series. Offensive line calls, to get the best blocking, are excellent. Proper blocking combinations are necessary and important for all series and, if the offense is going to set the "trap" against its opponent, they must be fully ready and prepared.

FORMATIONS AND PLAY SEQUENCES

Formations have much to do in attacking defenses. It must be remembered that only certain formations can utilize so many play sequences. It is important, therefore, for the coach to keep in mind what series he wants to utilize and from what formations; thus, he can best attack areas of a defense in better perspective.

In many cases, defenses will adjust to alignments with the change of different formations. If a series can be run from different formations, then the coach can find the formation where he can derive the best defensive alignment. With this, the coach can get better blocking combinations and running room for the ballcarrier.

The utilization of play sequences and formations can be grouped into five separate headings.

1. Numerous formations with minimum series.
2. Minimum formations with many series.
3. Many formations with numerous series.
4. Minimum formations with minimum series.
5. A combination of all.

Numerous Formations with Minimum Series

A few coaches throughout the nation desire as many formations as feasible while utilizing only a small number of play sequences. The reason for this is that coaches can drill series during their practice time with a minimum amount of time, work, and energy. However, they can give defenses different forms of sets, looks, and alignments. Coaches believe that by accomplishing this they can make defenses prepare longer against their particular formations and series since defenses must be able to adjust properly to all offensive sets.

Another important conclusion for numerous formations is that they grant the offense an advantage in locating a formation that will cause the defense to adjust improperly. Therefore, the offense will employ that particular formation more readily. There are coaches who devote hours upon hours on Sundays looking at their opponent's defense, but through films not their own. They continually check the formation being employed. In many instances they find a formation that would alter the defense slightly to their liking. The coaches would then adjust their play sequences to the formation. One coach who practices this every year happens to go to a bowl each season and has been successful year in and year out.

Minimum Formations with Many Series

There are coaches, however, who believe in only a few formations with many series. These coaches believe they will work with one or two formations only and attempt to attack defenses with their adjustments. The coaches will employ many play sequences and drill their teams to block all defensive maneuvers from the formations they utilize.

A good reason for minimum formations is that many series can be executed from the formations presented, while the players do not have to learn different positions from one play to the next. The players remain in one position most of the time. This is especially true for the backfield and receivers. The coaches assume, if a defense adjusts to the offensive formation to stop a particular series, the coach can utilize other play sequences to outmaneuver the defensive adjustments. If the defense changes, then the offense will alter the play sequences and execute something different.

Many Formations with Numerous Series

The philosophy for this offense is that it takes the strengths of many formations and numerous series to attack defensive coverages. The weakness, however, is that there remains a multitude for players to learn, study, and understand. Also, there must be enough time in the practice schedule to drill each segment of the offense. If this can be accomplished, though, it has the capability of a great attack. The defensive opponent must work twice as hard against all the plays and formations he will be facing in the game. This may take time away from the opponent's offensive attack if they do not platoon.

Minimum Formations with Minimum Series

The offense which includes very little formations and series utilizes the strength of each one. Many coaches employ this type of offense because of simplicity. It is very easy for the players to learn and the coach usually spends more time on fundamentals and techniques versus every defense. He believes strongly that blocking and tackling is going to win games during a season. While this strategy is good, it is also easy for the opponent's defensive team to prepare versus the offense. Since the defense is adjusting to very little, it can do anything necessary to stop the offensive plays executed.

A Combination of All

There are, of course, numerous coaches who employ a combination of a number of formations and play sequences. They utilize a well-balanced offensive attack. These coaches attempt to attack defenses with their adjustments and coverages by strategically using formations and series against defenses in the correct manner. While utilizing a well-balanced attack, the coach can find a formation that gets the best adjustments from the defense. He can utilize his play sequences strategically against the defensive coverages also. When the defense adjusts, the coach can then change his series or formation. The coach, therefore, has at his disposal more weapons to attack the defense. In a well-balanced attack, the coach does not have too *little* or too *many* formations and series. He has enough to strategically and intellectually outmaneuver the defensive opponent.

CLASSIFICATION OF OFFENSIVE FORMATIONS

Offensive formations can generally be classified into three areas.

1. Closed Formations
2. Balanced Formations
3. Wide Formations

Closed Formations

Diagram 1-1 illustrates a closed formation. This formation has everyone tight and there are no split ends, flankers, or wide slots. It includes a straight "T" backfield, a three-back I, wishbone, or possibly one wingback, etc. The following are the strengths and weaknesses of a closed formation:

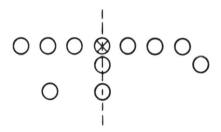

DIAGRAM 1-1
A Closed Formation

STRENGTHS

1. Strong inside.
2. Strong up the middle.
3. Good blocking off-tackle in both directions with two tight ends.
4. Good pass protection on pass plays.
5. Can counter and trap easily.
6. A great deal of faking can be accomplished with three backs.
7. It is an excellent running formation.
8. Single wing blocking can easily be accomplished.
9. If winged—good for reverses, extra blockers, etc.

WEAKNESSES

1. Cannot run outside as easily, unless winged.
2. Does not spread and widen defense.
3. Must have inside attack for formation to be effective.
4. It is not good for a passing attack.
5. Ends cannot release from the line of scrimmage as easily.

Balanced Formations

Diagram 1-2 illustrates a balanced formation. This type of formation employs at least one wide man to either side; this could be a flanker, split end, or wide slot. The opposite side is tight with a tight end, tight slot, wingback, etc. The following are the strengths and weaknesses of balanced formations:

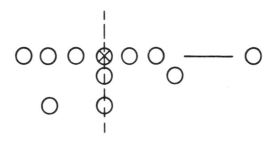

DIAGRAM 1-2
A Balanced Formation

STRENGTHS

1. There is a good tight attack to one side.
2. There is a good wide attack to the split side.
3. The formation spreads the defense to one side. It can get different defensive secondary coverages to this side.
4. It is both a good running and passing attack.
5. Split man can easily release from the line of scrimmage.
6. Can still get good counters, fakes, and reverses inside and outside.
7. It has all the advantages of both the closed and wide offensive formations.

WEAKNESSES

1. It does not employ two tight ends for blocking (if flanker—a good running back is eliminated).
2. Does not give as good an over-all passing attack as in wide formations.

Wide Formations

Wide formations include wide receivers on either side of the center. This includes either two split ends, two flankers, one split end and one flanker, and/or a combination of slots. Diagram 1-3 illustrates an example of a wide formation. The following are the strengths and weaknesses:

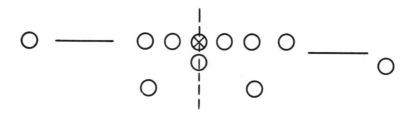

DIAGRAM 1-3
A Wide Formation

STRENGTHS

1. Spreads the defense wide to both sides.
2. Both receivers can release quickly off the line of scrimmage.
3. Different defensive secondary coverages can be attacked.
4. It is an excellent passing formation utilizing both drop-backs and sprint-outs to either side.

WEAKNESSES

1. Not an effective running game.
2. Not as effective running off-tackle to split end side.
3. Not as good a running attack with two offensive backs. If three offensive running backs, there is no tight end.
4. Not as effective (two backs) for fakes, counters, and reverses.

FORMATIONS WITH STRENGTHS, WEAKNESSES AND SERIES

The offensive formations that follow are some of the many sets that are seen throughout the country. Strengths and weaknesses are discussed with some of the play sequences that can be utilized successfully with each formation. While some series are not mentioned, many can still be employed.

The "T" Formation (Diagram 1-4)

DIAGRAM 1-4

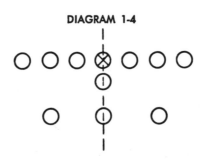

STRENGTHS

1. Middle and inside are strong.
2. Counters, traps, and faking available.
3. Can get good power blocking with the three backs.
4. With three backs, there is good protection for passes.
5. Excellent for a goal-line offense.
6. Good for coming out of the critical zone (danger area).

WEAKNESSES

1. Weak to the outside.
2. Not especially good for a passing attack.
3. Does not spread the defense for other possible exploitation.
4. Cannot get good releases from the line of scrimmage for the passing game.

SERIES OR PLAYS

1. Split "T," if formation widens.
2. Inside and outside belly.
3. Isolation and traps up the middle.
4. Power off-tackle.
5. Cross-buck with halfback and fullback.
6. Play action passes.
7. Possible sprint-out pass.

The Wing "T" Formation (Diagram 1-5)

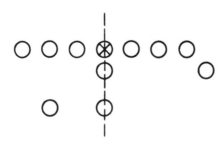

DIAGRAM 1-5

STRENGTHS

1. Same as "T" to weak side.
2. Wing is in good position for releasing on passes, blocking, and counter plays.

3. Stronger outside for running.
4. Better for passing to wing side.

WEAKNESSES

1. Defense is not wide enough.
2. Less faking occurs in the backfield.
3. Dive man taken away.

SERIES OR PLAYS

1. Inside and outside belly.
2. Power series.
3. Can sprint-out pass.
4. Split "T" to weak side.
5. Good for Delaware Wing "T."

Double Wing "T" (Diagram 1-6)

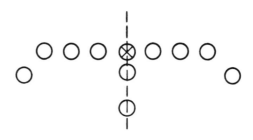

DIAGRAM 1-6

STRENGTHS

1. Four men on quick release on pass.
2. Can motion wingman back to halfback position. Defense cannot rotate one way or another.
3. More of a passing formation.

WEAKNESSES

1. Only one man in backfield for running.
2. Not much faking in the backfield.
3. Both dive men taken away.
4. Not a well-balanced formation for running.

SERIES OR PLAYS

1. Must have motion to get good series.
2. Good for both sprint-out and drop-back passing attack.

Wing "T"—Split End (Diagram 1-7)

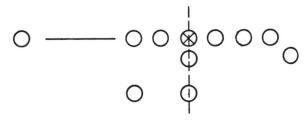

DIAGRAM 1-7

STRENGTHS

1. Same strength to the wing as Wing "T."
2. Split end widens the defense.
3. Better passing formation.
4. End can release quicker from line of scrimmage.
5. Split end has good outside-in angle block on the inside defensive people.

WEAKNESSES

1. Eliminates tight end off-tackle play.
2. Same weaknesses to wing as Wing "T."

SERIES OR PLAYS

1. Inside and outside belly.
2. Good quick pitch series with the split end.
3. Sprint-out or drop-back pass.
4. Good Split "T" option to weak side with the utilization of the split end.

Tight Slot (Diagram 1-8)

DIAGRAM 1-8

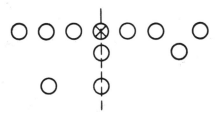

STRENGTHS

1. Same to weakside as "T" formation.
2. Same to slot as in Wing "T."
3. Since the tight end and back have switched this may give defensive talent difficulty in execution.
4. Tight end is in a quicker position to release from the line of scrimmage.
5. Slotback is in good position to block, run, and release for passes within the offensive system.

WEAKNESSES

1. Same weaknesses to weak side as in Split "T" or straight "T" attack.
2. Same weaknesses to slot side as in Wing "T" attack.

SERIES OR PLAYS

1. Same as Wing "T."

Wide Slot—Split Backfield (Diagram 1-9)

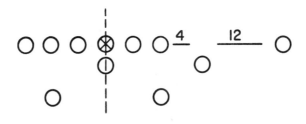

DIAGRAM 1-9

STRENGTHS

1. Strong to slot side.
2. Balanced enough to run to split side.
3. Excellent passing formation (two quick receivers to one side).
4. Two backs can release quickly on pass routes.
5. Good power to weak side with the alignment of the tight end.
6. Slot can both release quickly for the passing attack and can still be utilized in the running game.
7. The offensive formation spreads the defense well.

WEAKNESSES

1. No fullback for quick middle plays.

1. Sweeps and Power.
2. Good for cross-buck series.
3. Can quick pitch to both sides, excellent to slot side.
4. Good sprint-out and drop-back passing formation.
5. Quick dive plays are good.
6. Triple option can be run.

Pro Formation (Diagram 1-10)

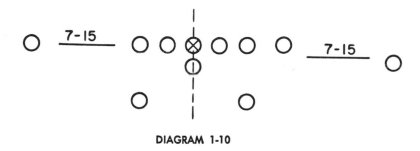

DIAGRAM 1-10

STRENGTHS

1. Excellent passing formation.
2. Two receivers can release quickly from the line of scrimmage on either side of the center.
3. Widens and spreads defense considerably. The running game may execute better because of this.
4. Two offensive backs are in good position to release for passes also.
5. Well-balanced running formation to either side of the center.
6. Both wide men can angle block to the inside for the offensive running game.

WEAKNESSES

1. Only two offensive backs can run with the football.
2. Not as much faking in the backfield can occur because of this.
3. No fullback for an up-the-middle threat versus the defensive opponent.

SERIES OR PLAYS

1. Excellent for drop-back passes (three, four, or five men release).
2. Sweep series.
3. Cross-buck series.
4. Quick pitch series.

5. Quick dive plays.

6. Triple option series.

Single Wing (Diagram 1-11)

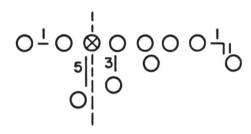

DIAGRAM 1-11

STRENGTHS

1. Makes the defense adjust to an unbalanced line.

2. Very strong to the wing side.

3. Powerful—two backs in position to block to one side.

4. Can get to the weak side quickly.

5. Good for passes, with four men on the line to release quickly. Passer is set and in good position to release the football.

6. Excellent kicking formation (quick kick).

WEAKNESSES

1. Not as deceptive as with a "T" quarterback formation.

2. Not as much power to weak side.

3. Offensive center must be accurate on the snap.

4. Protection is unbalanced for the passer.

5. Must have good tailback who can run, pass, and kick.

SERIES OR PLAYS

1. The spin series.

2. The power series.

3. The buck lateral series.

4. The drop-back pass series (quarterback or passer is ready to pass the ball).

5. Reverses and counters are excellent versus over-shifted defense to strong side.

Double Wing (Diagram 1-12)

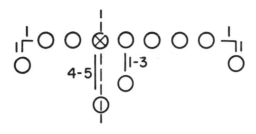

DIAGRAM 1-12

STRENGTHS

1. Unbalanced line may cause the defense problems.
2. Four quick men to release on passes.
3. More balanced formation than the Single Wing.
4. Two runners are in the backfield.
5. Passer is in excellent position to pass the ball.
6. Good for counters and reverses.
7. Good inside and outside running attack.
8. Good for the kicking game (quick kick).

WEAKNESSES

1. Not as powerful to the strong side as in the Single Wing formation.
2. Not as deceptive as the "T" formation.
3. Must have good tailback who can run, pass, and kick the football.
4. Center must snap the ball with accuracy.

SERIES OR PLAYS

1. Spin series.
2. Power series.
3. Good for reverses and counters.
4. Drop-back passes—passer in position.

Short Punt (Diagram 1-13)

DIAGRAM 1-13

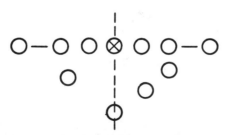

STRENGTHS

1. Strong to the inside.
2. Can get outside adequately.
3. It is a good, balanced formation.
4. Three or four men can release on passes quickly.
5. Passer is in good position to throw the ball.
6. Great deal of faking can be accomplished in the backfield.
7. Good protection for the passer with good release for the receivers.

WEAKNESSES

1. Not as strong to weak side.
2. Center must snap the ball accurately.
3. Tailback must be a good runner, passer and kicker.
4. Not as deceptive as the "T" formation.

SERIES OR PLAYS

1. Spinner series.
2. Power series.
3. Drop-back series.
4. Good for counter plays.

Shotgun Formation (Diagram 1-14)

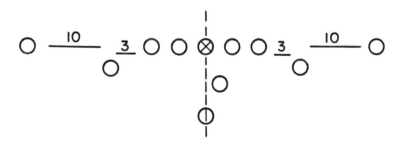

DIAGRAM 1-14

STRENGTHS

1. The formation spreads and widens the defense considerably.
2. Two quick receivers can release from the line of scrimmage quickly.
3. Four possible receivers on passes.
4. Excellent kicking formation.

WEAKNESSES

1. Not as good protection for the passer.
2. Not a good running formation.
3. Must have a good passer.

SERIES OR PLAYS

1. Good drop-back pass series (quarterback ready, in position).
2. Possible reverses and counters can be used.

Side Saddle "T" (Diagram 1-15)

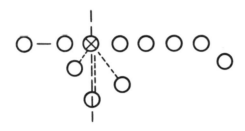

DIAGRAM 1-15

STRENGTHS

1. The formation attempts to get a combination of "T" and Single Wing attack.
2. A great deal of faking can be accomplished.
3. Powerful to strong side.
4. Can get outside quick to weak side.
5. Confusion will result on who might get the ball.
6. Good quick kick formation.

WEAKNESSES

1. Fumbles may occur with the quarterback-center exchange.
2. Must have a good center for the snap.
3. Deception may be lost due to the quarterback position.

SERIES OR PLAYS

1. Power and sweep series.
2. Spinner series.
3. Counter and reverse plays are available.

2

The Green Bay Pro Sweep

The Green Bay Pro Sweep is one of the most famous power sweep plays executed in football today. While virtually all pro teams employ the play, it is known as the Green Bay Sweep due to its popularity while the Green Bay professional football team was under the leadership of Coach Vince Lombardi. During these years Coach Lombardi gained and received great success with it.

THE PRO FORMATION AND THE SWEEP PLAY

Another reason it is known as the pro sweep is due to the popular wide formation the sweep is employed with. Since a good passing game requires wide people, usually most coaches utilize the pro formation (Diagram 2-1).

However, a good running game is necessary and required. Therefore, a sweep is needed to attack the outside areas of the defensive perimeter. The sweep had to be blocked differently, due to the width of the players (receivers) in the pro formation, and the sweep was envisioned. There would be no double-teaming at the point of attack as there are in other power plays. Once the sweep has been feared other companionable plays can be executed with greater ease.

DIAGRAM 2-1
The Basic Pro Formation with a Split Backfield

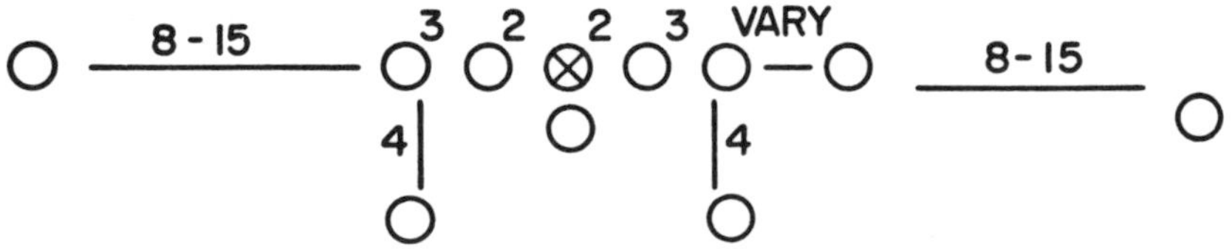

The Strengths of the Pro Sweep

The strengths of the Green Bay Pro Sweep are many and the following are the important points to remember:

1. Gets outside with power and speed with the utilization of wide formations.
2. The sweep can go outside or inside according to the play of the defensive end.
3. It is good if the defensive end is waiting and floating or crashing hard to the inside.
4. The sweep does not require double-team blocking or power blocking.
5. Splitting by the tight end causes alignment adjustments by the defense; this causes weaknesses from the original basic defense.
6. If the defense is stunting inside, the offense can go outside with the sweep.

A Word on Execution

Running the pro sweep takes more at times than good personnel. Teamwork with proper execution is necessary and most important. The sweep itself is a highly skilled play which utilizes a great deal of keying and reading. The tight end must read the maneuvers of the defensive end or linebacker; both guards must read the end's block, while the tailback must key the movements of the guard. One false move or an improper "read" can cause failure without gaining yardage.

The important points of execution for the pro sweep are as follows:

1. The block by the tight end.
2. The block by the fullback on the inside defensive men.
3. The crack-back block or the seal of the flanker back.
4. The onside and offside guards pull and the blocking on the corner.
5. The tailback's ability to read the tight end and guard's block.
6. The execution of the quarterback: proper steps, good hand-off, and a great fake on the bootleg.

Formations Necessary

The Green Bay Sweep is usually better utilized when employing wide formations to the side of the sweep. It should be remembered, the sweep can be run to the tight end side and away (split end, etc.). It is necessary to have a split backfield also. The block of the fullback (or halfback) over the offensive tackle area, and the relationship needed for the hand-off between the quarterback and ballcarrier requires it. Diagram 2-2 and 2-3 illustrate two offensive formations the pro sweep can be executed from.

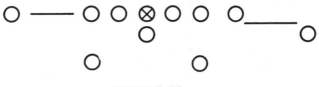

DIAGRAM 2-2
The Pro Formation

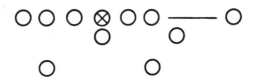

DIAGRAM 2-3
The Slot Formation

THE PLAY OF THE GREEN BAY PRO SWEEP

Diagram 2-4 indicates the Green Bay Sweep versus the 6-1 defense (sometimes thought of as the 4-3 defense). (Other defenses are illustrated in diagrams 2-5A through 2-6B to illustrate the blocking rules.) Following are the rules, execution, and coaching points of the pro sweep.

DIAGRAM 2-4
The Pro Sweep

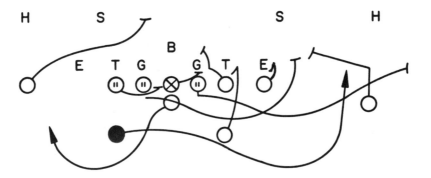

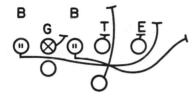

DIAGRAM 2-5A
5-4 Look

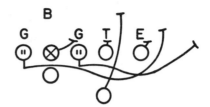

DIAGRAM 2-5B
6-1 Look

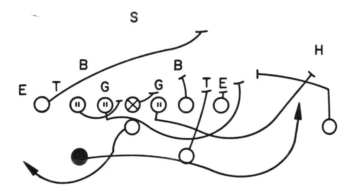

DIAGRAM 2-6A
Versus a Wide Tackle-6 Defense

DIAGRAM 2-6B
Versus a Split-6 Defense

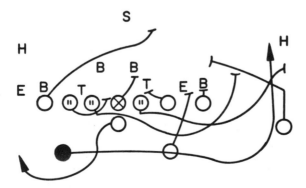

OFFENSIVE LINE

Tight End

Rule: Over, inside, near linebacker.

Execution: Split approximately four yards. Make the defensive end play inside or head-up. Create a maneuver not favorable to the defense with the "nasty split." Do not let the defender make penetration more than one yard.

Aligned Inside—If aligned to the inside, block down hard, cutting off any penetration such as a forcing maneuver. Take a lead step, then a cross-over one.

Aligned Head-Up—If the defensive man is aligned head-up, put weight on inside leg and take a quick set position. Make the defensive man commit. If he goes to the inside, screen him off. If he takes an out-maneuver, force him to the outside.

Coaching Points: The offensive end must stop penetration. He should vary the split and see how the defensive man adjusts. Do not over-extend the body with the block being executed. Take the defensive man anywhere he desires to go.

Onside Tackle

Rule: Inside, gap, linebacker.

Execution: Read the defense and make proper block. If defensive man is to the inside, stop penetration first, then pursuit. If blocking a linebacker, stop his pursuit course and cut him off.

Coaching Points: The tackle should be aggressive and should fire-out hard at his opponent. If the linebacker cannot be blocked, make a possible switch with the fullback's block.

Onside Guard

Rule: Pull and kick out beyond the end's block.

Execution: From a good three-point stance, the guard should execute a good pull maneuver. The first step is deep with following steps gaining depth into the backfield. The guard should look to the corner and kick out the first man that shows. If no defender comes quick, then turn up and block most dangerous man that shows.

Coaching Points: Snap head and arm on first initial move to get outside. First step should not be long, but back. Be quick and get to outside fast.

Center

Rule: Onside, over.

Execution: Make a good proper snap and take a cross-over step in the direction of the ballcarrier. Block to onside and prevent any penetration by the defensive man. If man is aligned over, center can either block to onside hard or take middle guard if dangerous.

Coaching Points: Look for stunts over onside guard area and stop penetration. Move quick and fast. Attempt to get head on other side of defensive man to cut off pursuit.

Offside Guard

Rule: On gap, pull and seal.

Execution: If a defensive man is aligned in the inside gap, block him and prevent penetration. If no man is stationed there, pull and get depth. If the corner cannot be made, then turn upfield in the first hole that shows. Look to the inside and seal off pursuit.

Coaching Points: The first step should be deep on the pull. Read the block of the tight end as depth is made. Go inside or outside according to the block executed.

Offside Tackle

Rule: Pull and wall off center area.

Execution: Pull hard and quick. Step down the line and seal anything off. If a defensive player does not penetrate, then fire downfield and pick up the play.

Coaching Points: Do not get depth on the pull. Read the defense for the defensive man that may have to be blocked. It is important to look for stunts in the middle area also.

Split End

Rule: Release and block middle ⅓.

Execution: Release to the inside hard. Sprint and chop anything down that shows in the middle ⅓ area.

Coaching Points: It is possible to run a pass route if the quarterback is faking the bootleg. If blocking the ⅓ area, get there quickly and throw a block. Do not look for the ballcarrier—he will find you.

BACKFIELD

Flanker or Wide Back

Rule: Block number 2 man in secondary.

Execution: On the snap of the ball, release from the line of scrimmage and attempt to drive the defensive halfback back. Quickly look to the inside and block the inside fill man (either an inside safety in the 4-deep or the safety man in the 3-deep). If the 3-deep safety does not show, then seal off any inside pursuit. When the defensive man comes, be in a good ready position to hit the opponent. Square the feet, stay low with head up and chop man down.

Coaching Points: Attempt to get a straight release before going to the inside. The flanker may have to go to the inside on the first step due to the alignment of the defense. The alignment of the flanker can be close, near, or far due to the defensive setup and the type of team playing, etc.

Fullback

Rule: Drive on the first man outside the offensive tackle.

Execution: Explode forward and go directly to the defensive man in the area. Chop the opponent down. Do not throw too quickly and miss the defender. Aim head for the outside knee and cut him off.

Coaching Points: Do not come up, but stay low. Put face in tough. If linebacker, block higher.

Quarterback

Execution: Reverse pivot at twelve o'clock and hand the ball off to the tailback. Continue on course and fake the bootleg. Read the defensive secondary for its coverage.

Coaching Points: Keep ball in close to belly. Look the ball into the ballcarrier's stomach. Get depth after hand-off. Do not look back at ballcarrier.

Tailback

Execution: Ballcarrier—From a good offensive stance, employ a cross-over step initially. Take the hand-off from the quarterback. On the third step, start getting depth and read the block of the offensive end. If blocked in, go out; and if blocked out, run inside. Follow the blocks of the offensive guards and come up the line of scrimmage with shoulders square. Run for daylight.

Coaching Points: Do not lean and indicate direction of the flow. Must make a quick "read" and continue for daylight. Make a quick decision and keep body under control.

Variations of Blocking Schemes

In many cases, due to alignments, defenses, or personnel differences, the blocking rules will not work effectively. Therefore, certain alterations must be made to attack the defense in gaining the best yardage.

Diagram 2-7 illustrates the wide man or flankerback coming down hard on the defensive end while the tight end blocks to the inside. This is accomplished when the tight end cannot handle his man and the offensive calls for a different blocking maneuver.

DIAGRAM 2-7

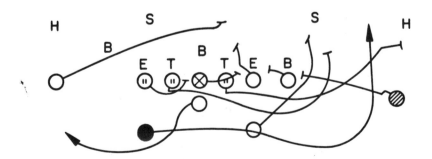

Another blocking pattern was explained previously. If the offensive tackle cannot release on the linebacker versus a certain defense, the tackle will take the fullback's assignment while the fullback blocks on the linebacker.

Diagram 2-8 indicates a blocking change-up with the offensive center and tackle. In this case, if the offensive center cannot block onside (because the defensive man on the offensive guard moves outside to quickly), the offensive tackle can block down while the center releases for the linebacker.

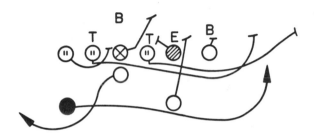

DIAGRAM 2-8

On the offside, when there is a defensive man aligned in the center-guard gap, the offensive guard cannot pull. However, the offside tackle can take his assignment and pull around the end. If the coach decides to employ this coaching point, he must drill the offensive tackle on the pull and proper depth maneuver. He should coordinate with the onside guard and running tailback also (Diagram 2-9).

Vince Lombardi, in his book *Run to Daylight,* mentions a brief history and a few techniques about the pro sweep. He states:

> Right end—drive that man over you in the direction of his angle. Never allow penetration to the inside or over you hard. If he penetrates inside he knocks off both our pulling guards. Your eyes and your weight should be to the inside. If he comes to the inside he takes a big gamble. If he goes to the outside you set and don't make your move until he's past your nose and then drive—drive—drive him to the sideline.
>
> Right tackle and fullback—you work as a unit, responsible for the left end and middle linebacker. For a sweep to be successful you can't have penetration by the defensive end. Tackle—drive the end unless he is outside of you. If he's outside, slam, and set yourself up in the seal position and seal inside. Fullback—drive the first man outside your tackle, and you can't

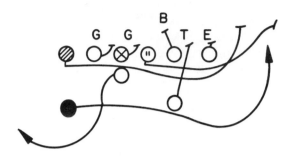

DIAGRAM 2-9

make a curved or circle approach to that man. Speed is absolutely necessary for the first guard, the onside guard, to clear. If none outside your tackle, if the tackle has taken him, seal inside for the middle linebacker.

First guard—the onside right guard must pull hard to clear the fullback's move. Ninety-five percent of the time you will pull outside your onside end. Center—cut off that left tackle onside, because he'll have nobody over him. This is one of the two toughest blocks involved, but you must make it. Second guard—the off-side left guard must pull hard, look for the hole and seal to the inside. Offside tackle—the left tackle must cut off the defensive right tackle. He'll also have nobody over him and you must pull like a guard. This is the second of the two toughest blocks, because you must take him where you find him, whether he comes across that line or whether he slides with the play. You must block him. Flanker—take the left safety man, wherever he is. Halfback—come hard until you get the ball from the quarterback. Make a little belly-out and then wing! That's it.[1]

The Split End Sweep

The sweep to the split end side is similar to the pro sweep that was previously explained. In this case the tight end is not utilized. Diagram 2-10 illustrates the split end sweep with the rules similar to the tight end play. Notice the tight end can pull and seal the offensive tackle area if necessary.

---

[1] Vince Lombardi, *Run to Daylight* (Englewood Cliffs, N.Y.: Prentice-Hall, Inc., 1963) pp. 106–107.

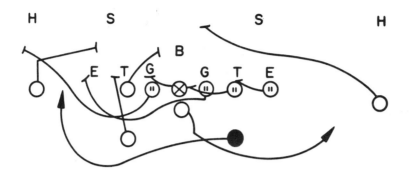

DIAGRAM 2-10
The Split End Sweep

The Off-Tackle Power

When the defense adjusts to stop the pro sweep, the offense must counteract with other plays and blocking schemes to attack the defense also. It should be remembered, a play's value is not only in *that one play* itself, but also in the counter that sets it up.

The power off-tackle play is shown in Diagram 2-11. As can be seen, the play starts out and looks similar to the sweep, except that the fullback fakes toward the tackle area and kicks the defensive end out. The tight end can either block down on the defensive tackle, release to seal a linebacker off inside, or he can drive the defensive secondary deep.

DIAGRAM 2-11

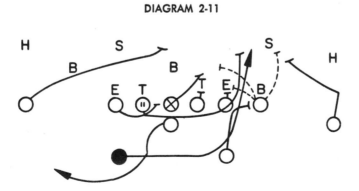

The Trap Off-Tackle

One of the finest counter's from the pro sweep is the trap off-tackle. It begins exactly like the sweep, except that the defensive man being blocked by the fullback is now influenced by the fullback and trapped by the offside guard. It is an excellent trap play that takes a good deal of timing between the offensive linemen and backfield. The offensive guard pulls and traps the first man over to outside the offensive tackle. Diagram 2-12 illustrates the trap versus the 5-4 Oklahoma.

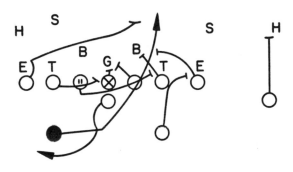

DIAGRAM 2-12
Versus the 5-4 Oklahoma

The Middle Trap

Diagram 2-13 indicates a trap attacking the middle. It is a quick, short trap by the offside guard. The quarterback reverse pivots and coordinates an inside hand-off with the tailback. The ballcarrier executes the same cross-over technique, but on the third step pushes toward the middle area following the guard's trap block.

DIAGRAM 2-13

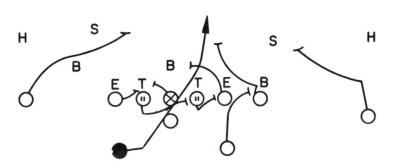

The Off-Tackle Counter Trap

The counter off-tackle trap is an excellent counter from the sweep play (Diagram 2-14). The fullback steps toward the off-tackle area, pushes off his outside foot, and cuts to the offside. The tailback fakes the sweep maneuver. The quarterback reverse pivots as if to give to the tailback and initiates an inside hand-off with the fullback.

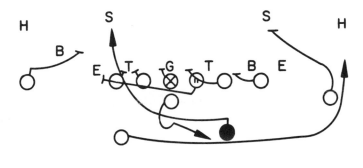

DIAGRAM 2-14

The Middle Counter Trap

Diagram 2-15 illustrates the counter trap through the middle area. The trap with its fundamentals and techniques are similar to the off-tackle trap except that the play attacks up the middle.

DIAGRAM 2-15

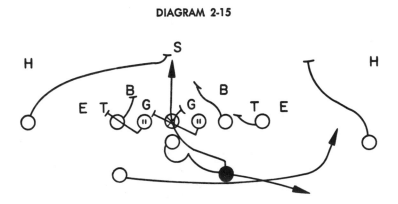

The Flanker Reverse

While reverses are used sparingly in a game or throughout the season, they are a necessary part of any winning sequence of plays. Diagram 2-16 illustrates a flanker reverse. On the snap of the ball, the quarterback reverse pivots and hands the ball to the tailback. The two guards execute a reverse pull (pulling in one direction and reversing their field), while the tailback hands back to the flankerback. The offside peels back on any defensive pursuit.

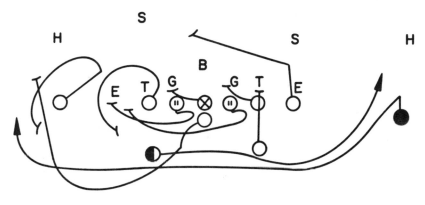

DIAGRAM 2-16

Play Action Sweep Passes

To keep the defense off-balance, play action passes are good and necessary. Diagram 2-17A indicates a fake to the tailback with the quarterback rolling toward the flow. Another play action pass is the halfback pass. It can be run exactly as the quarterback play action pass; however, the quarterback fakes the bootleg (Diagram 2-17B).

DIAGRAM 2-17A

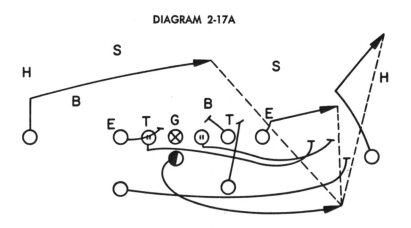

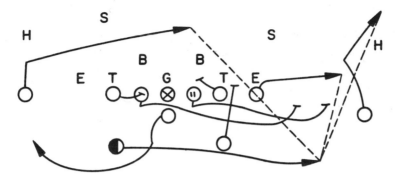

DIAGRAM 2-17B

Another effective pro sweep pass can be executed as shown in Diagram 2-17C with a three-man pattern to the onside. The quarterback can either roll to the flow or drop straight back. Any combination of pass patterns can be employed with the fake of the sweep.

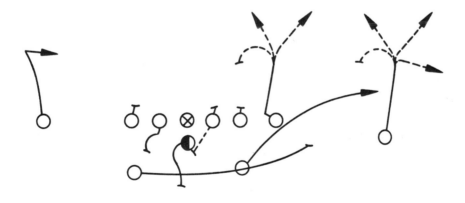

DIAGRAM 2-17C

The Bootleg

With the bootleg, the quarterback fakes to the tailback and continues to the outside. He can either pull up and hit the split end, trailing end, or throw back to his secondary receivers (Diagram 2-18). The bootleg can be utilized toward the tight end side also.

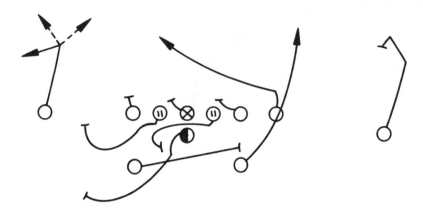

DIAGRAM 2-18

Play Action from the Middle Trap

Diagram 2-19 indicates a play action pass coming off of the middle trap play. In this case, the quarterback fakes the tailback hand-off and continues outside for the pass.

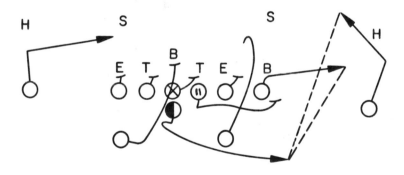

DIAGRAM 2-19

Throwback to the Quarterback

The quarterback hands the ball to the tailback and continues on as if faking the bootleg. The ballcarrier starts his sweep course, but stops and throws back to the quarterback looking over his inside shoulder (Diagram 2-20). The offensive guards employ a reverse pull and the split end and tackle peel back to the inside.

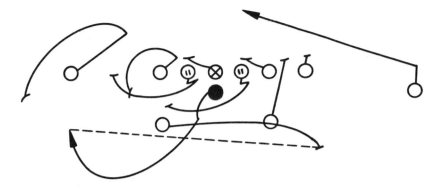

DIAGRAM 2-20

The Power Series

Power, defined by Webster's Seventh New Collegiate Dictionary is "a force of armed men; a large number or quantity; physical might; force; strength;" etc.[1]

A definition of power in a football series, therefore, would consist of a large number of men or force (physical might) at the point of attack. This is what a coach attempts to employ—*power,* with as much force as can be mustered to gain the advantage. As is well known throughout history, military strategists have used the quantity of men over weaker and lesser foes to win the battle. In this case, it's brawn before brain.

What Is a Power Series?

The power series in football is quite different than the Green Bay Sweep. The pro sweep required wide formations. The power series needs more players at the point of attack, and therefore, tighter formations are usually necessary. With a power play or series there is usually a two-on-one block at one of the defensive positions at the attack area. A three-on-two situation may result. However, a four-on-two situation can occur also. This is not saying that one or more players are leading through the hole at one time or another.

It must be remembered that within the power series other plays coming off the basic play can be used. This can be different fakes and counters with straight, cross, trap blocking, etc., being employed.

Strengths of a Power Series

Utilizing a power series can be a great advantage to the football coach.

---

[1] *Webster's Seventh New Collegiate Dictionary* (Springfield, Mass.: G. & C. Merriam Co., p. 666.

The following are the strengths of the power sequence of plays:

1. Usually very easy to execute and simple to learn.
2. A great deal of mistakes can be eliminated due to less faking and ballhandling in the backfield.
3. A 2-on-1 or 3-on-1, or more, exists at the point of attack, creating more power in the area.
4. Offensive backs and linemen leading through the hole help for blocking power in the running lane beyond the line of scrimmage.
5. Offensive linemen are waiting and floating on the line of scrimmage and not causing or attempting penetration.
6. Power is good inside when a defense is set up for the outside game and vice versa; when a defense attempts to stop the offense inside.
7. The power series is excellent when going in for a score and the defense jams up hard to stop the touchdown.
8. Power is necessary when coming out of the end zone and in the critical area where mistakes must be kept to a minimum.

Varied Formations

The type of play utilized will, in many cases, determine the formation. Numerous formations can be used with a power series. In most instances, at least one end will be tight on the line, with the two or three backs positioned somewhat tight also. It must be remembered, many different formations can be set with virtually the same form of blocking schemes and backfield maneuvers employed. With the different looks, only slight changes are usually necessary. Diagrams 3-1A to 3-1C illustrate a few of the formations that can be used for the utilization of power.

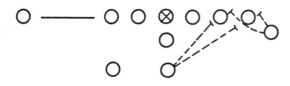

DIAGRAM 3-1A
The Wing "T" Formation

DIAGRAM 3-1B
The Three-Back "I" Formation

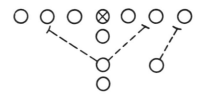

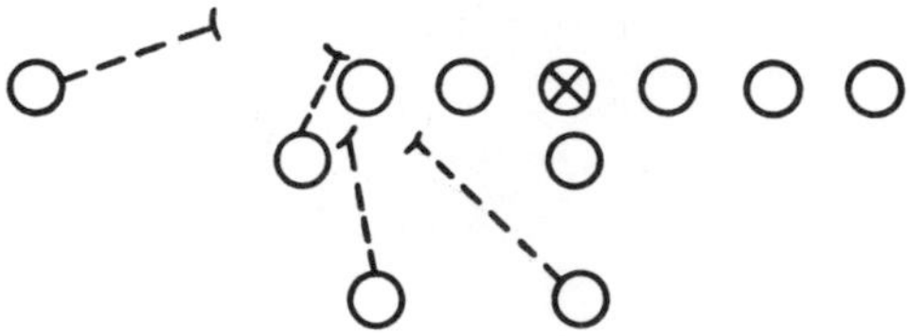

DIAGRAM 3-1C
The Strong-Slot Formation

Power Blocking Schemes

Blocking combinations for the power off-tackle hole can be numerous. Since there are many defenses with different adjustments, stunts, angles, etc., certain blocking combinations and patterns must be drilled and used. The same holds true for power plays up the middle areas.

Diagrams 3-2A to 3-2E show the many combinations of blocking on the line of scrimmage at the off-tackle hole versus the popular defenses. The blocking does not include off-side linemen or extra backs at the point of attack.

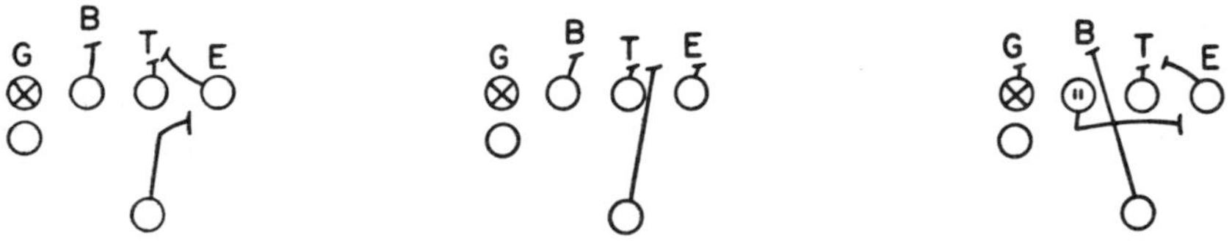

DIAGRAM 3-2A
Blocking Versus the 5-4 Oklahoma Defense

DIAGRAM 3-2B
Blocking Versus the 4-3 Defense

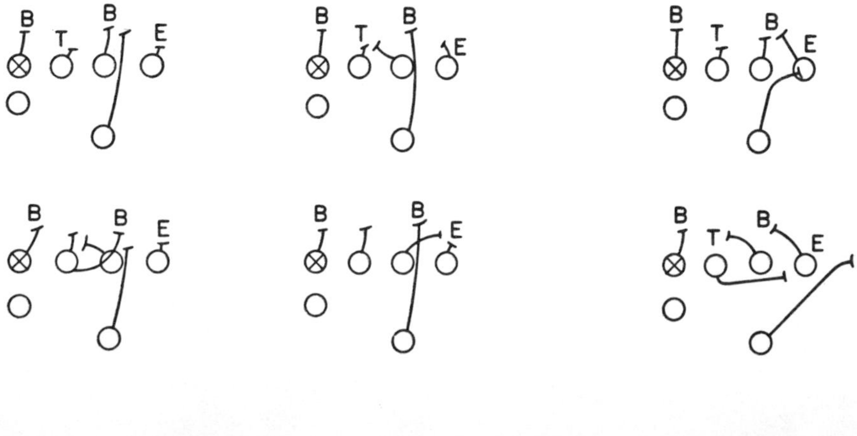

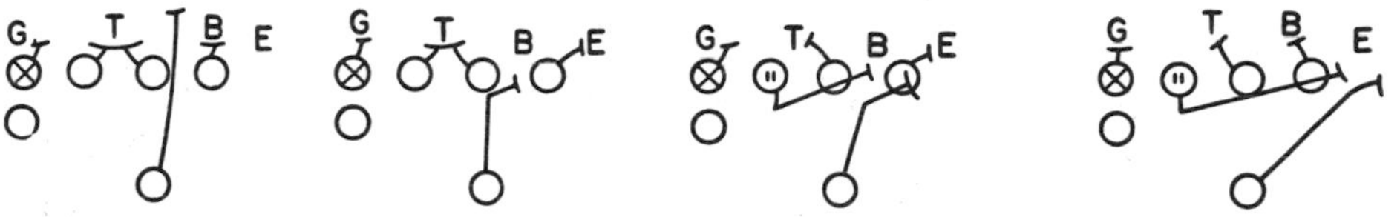

DIAGRAM 3-2C
Blocking Versus the Eagle-5 Defense

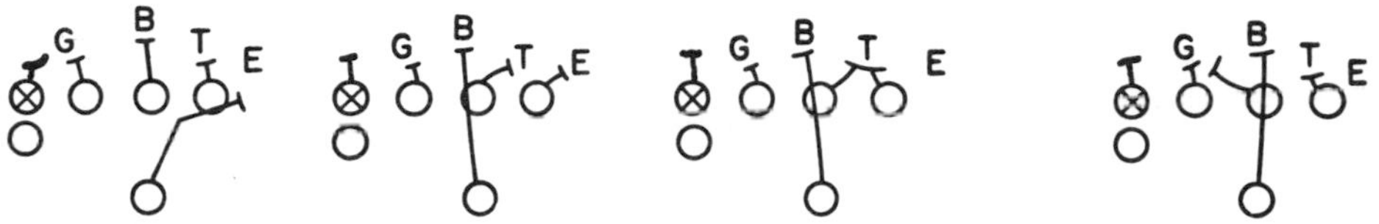

DIAGRAM 3-2D
Blocking Versus the Wide Tackle-6 Defense

DIAGRAM 3-2E
Blocking Versus the 4-4 or Split-6 Defense

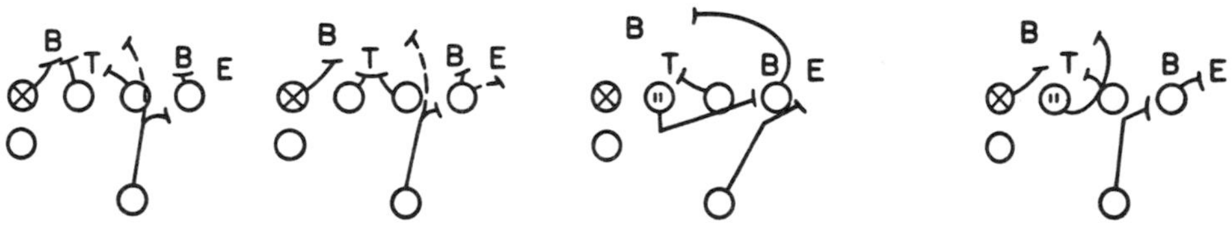

THE POWER OFF-TACKLE PLAY

There are numerous types and styles of power plays. The basic reason is that formations make a play and its series look different. However, most power plays and their sequence of plays are approximately the same with little difference. Diagram 3-3 illustrates a familiar power off-tackle play with the rules, execution and coaching points mentioned. Other power plays and series will be indicated throughout the chapter.

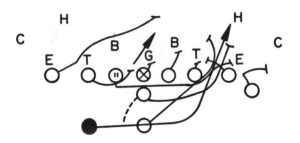

DIAGRAM 3-3
An Off-Tackle Power Play

OFFENSIVE LINE

Tight End

Rule: Over, inside.

Execution: Lead step to the hip of the defensive tackle. Drive the head in and slide to the outside. Make good contact and do not go to the ground. Keep a wide firm base with the feet.

Coaching Points: Do not turn the man down the line, but keep drive going at a 45 degree angle. If a man is in the gap, stop penetration first, then cut off pursuit.

Onside Tackle

Rule: Block number 2 (unless call dictates otherwise).

Execution: Step for the defensive man where he is and slide head where the hole is located. If double-team blocking, the tackle is the post blocker. Do not allow any penetration. Ground hands and feet and, when end makes contact, slide the hips to the offensive end's hips and drive-post block at a 45 degree angle down the line of scrimmage.

Coaching Points: Head goes directly in the middle on post block, then slide to inside when offensive end makes contact.

Onside Guard

Rule: Block number 1—listen for "Odd" or "Even" call by center.

Execution: Block the number 1 man from center area. Step in the direction of the play and make a good fire-out drive block. Cut the defensive man off to the inside.

Coaching Points: Execute good contact while driving feet. Do not go to the ground. If a linebacker is positioned over, take a good cut-off angle and chop linebacker down. If chopping is impossible, then drive the linebacker past the hole.

Center

Rule: Number 0, front stack, back gap, off-side linebacker.

Execution: Block Rule—If a defensive man is in the back gap, step with near foot and put head in front to eliminate penetration. This is a most important block due to the off-side guard pulling. If there is no man in the gap, block the linebacker and cut him down.

Coaching Points: If front stack occurs in gap, center must stop penetration also. Treat this as an "odd" defense. Stop penetration, then attempt to cut off pursuit angle of defensive opponent.

Offside Guard

Rule: Pull and seal at hole.

Execution: From a good offensive stance, execute a proper pull technique (snap head, arm, and foot) and come down staying as close as possible to the line of scrimmage. Run for tackle's butt and keep the back as near to a blocking position as possible. When turning up through the hole, plant the outside foot, lower the inside shoulder, pick up grass with the inside hand and come through the hole at a perpendicular angle. Block the first man that shows.

Coaching Points: Be quick and aggressive. Do not lean in the direction of the pull. On the first step, do not over-extend yourself. Run hard, but stay low to block any defender near the hole.

Offside Tackle

Rule: Seal-fire.

Execution: On the snap of the ball, step down hard and seal any man or stunting lineman/linebacker in the area. If no defensive man shows, then fire downfield and pick off any off-color jersey.

Coaching Points: If there is no man over the offensive guard, tackle can seal, but can turn back on defensive tackle originally positioned over him. If going downfield, stay close to the line of scrimmage and then come up on the defenders (Diagram 3-4).

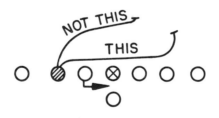

DIAGRAM 3-4

Offside End

Rule: Crossfield.

Execution: Before going crossfield, step down to the inside and slam man positioned over offensive tackle. Continue on a crossfield maneuver, staying near to the line of scrimmage. Throw a cross-body block at the defender.

Coaching Points: Do not look at the ballcarrier, but look for the enemy. Throw cross-body block at defensive man high. Throw punch at face as if to hit him and then come down through the defensive man.

OFFENSIVE BACKFIELD

Wingback

Rule: Fake 3, block 4.

Execution: Fake down to the inside on number 3 defensive man as if blocking for a sweep play, then push off on the inside foot and block the number 4 man. Screen this man off so that he cannot tackle to the inside. If number 4 man stunts hard, pick him off.

Coaching Points: Stay low on fake so a good blocking base will result when turning back to the outside. Keep a wide base with the head up.

Fullback

Execution: On the snap of the ball, take a lead step in the direction of the play and run for an aiming point of one foot outside the onside tackle's foot, and block he first man that shows. Take him to the outside. Look for the defensive end, but any man can come. Drive head in middle and attempt to knock the defender back. Slide the head to the inside.

Coaching Points: If a defender in the off-tackle area comes down at a hard, sharp angle, block the man in with a good inside shoulder block.

Quarterback

Execution: Take the ball from center, perform a ¾ reverse pivot and pitch the ball back to the tailback. Continue down the line and aim for the off-tackle hole. Drive up through area and block first defender that shows.

Coaching Points: Pitch the ball out with an underhand motion. Once pitch has been executed, start to get low for a good blocking base. Go hard for the hole.

Tailback

Execution: From a good offensive stance, execute a cross-over lead step in the direction of the flow. On the lead step, ball will be entering the hands. Take a firm grip and tuck away. Plant after the lead step and start to gain ground. Key guard's block and look for daylight.

Coaching Points: Run hard with knees high. Do not slow down through hole. If inches are needed for a first down, go hard to the hole and do not look for a cut. If first down is not needed, look for daylight. Be a runner.

Variations of the Power Play

There can be numerous variations to the power play indicated in Diagram 3-3. For an example, the coach can utilize the wingback through the hole being run rather than using him to block outside. Diagram 3-5 shows the wing slamming through the hole looking for a defender.

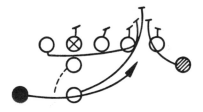

DIAGRAM 3-5

Another example is to eliminate the quarterback from any unnecessary blocking, but utilizing him on a bootleg fake or play action fake to the onside (Diagram 3-6).

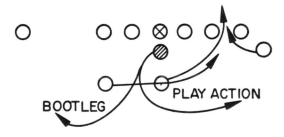

BOOTLEG   PLAY ACTION

DIAGRAM 3-6

The offside line, instead of going crossfield, could pull down the line as another change-up in the power play. Diagram 3-7 illustrates this offensive maneuver.

DIAGRAM 3-7

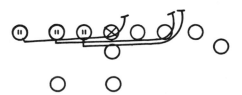

Formations can dictate a style of play and power also. A favorite off-tackle play today is employed from the "I" formation with a possibility of a guard pulling. Diagram 3-8 indicates a power off-tackle from an "I" formation. The "I" puts the tailback in a quicker position to get to the hole and it also gives him an opportunity to cut back and look for daylight.

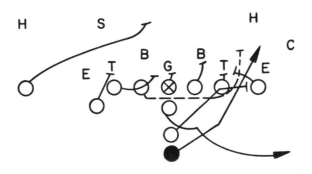

DIAGRAM 3-8

The "T" and the three-back "I" formations can be utilized also. From these formations power can be employed extensively, because of the positioning of the three offensive backs. A tremendous power play can be used from these formations and double-teaming can be accomplished on both sides of the hole. Diagrams 3-9 to 3-11 illustrate a three-back "I" formation with a power sequence of plays. Double-team blocking is used on either side of the hole in each instance. Diagram 3-12 shows a similar play away from the strength of the formation. Counters and traps can easily be employed with this type of power series.

DIAGRAM 3-9
Power Off-Tackle

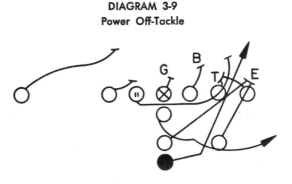

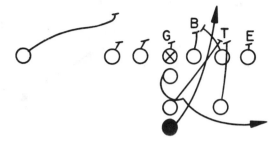

DIAGRAM 3-10
Power Off-Guard

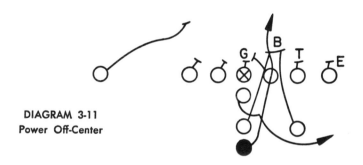

DIAGRAM 3-11
Power Off-Center

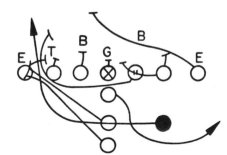

DIAGRAM 3-12
Power Off-Tackle Away From Strength

Penn State's Off-Tackle Play

Joe Paterno, Head Football Coach at Penn State University, sent the following off-tackle power play from a split backfield. Penn State ran this play from their power series with great success helping them onto their long winning streak. Diagram 3-13A shows the play versus the 5-4; Diagram 3-13B against the Split-6.

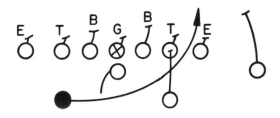

DIAGRAM 3-13A
Versus 5-4 Defense

DIAGRAM 3-13B
Versus Split-6 Defense

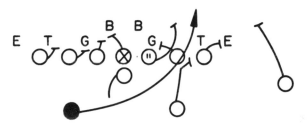

The lead back (blocker) runs for the inside leg of the offensive tackle and reads the tackle's block (or the defense if he recognizes it). The following is the offensive back's rule:

If the tackle blocks down—back blocks out.
If the tackle blocks out—back leads through and looks for the linebacker.
If the tackle blocks straight—back looks to help where needed in tackle's area.

The ballcarrier's initial course is for the tail of the offensive tackle. After receiving the ball from the quarterback, he should square up, keep his shoulders parallel to the line of scrimmage, and run for daylight. He should get up into and across the line of scrimmage before making a cut.

The Power Sweep

One of the plays employed most extensively from the power sequence is the sweep. It is destined to look as if it is hitting off-tackle, but runs outside. Diagram 3-14 illustrates the power sweep. The double-team block on the defensive end or number three man is the key to the play. With the power off-tackle play, the wingback faked on the defensive end and hit to the outside. On the sweep, however, he is driving the defensive end to the inside. The fullback aims for one foot outside the block of the double-team and chops the first defender that shows. If the defensive man contains, then the fullback should kick him out.

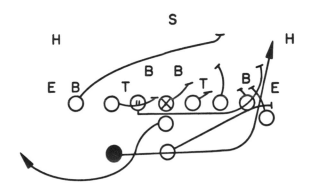

DIAGRAM 3-14
The Power Sweep

Another power sweep is indicated in Diagram 3-15 from a "T" formation versus a 5-4 Oklahoma defense. In this case, both guards are pulling, the quarterback pitches the ball and helps lead the play. John M. Yovicsin, the successful Coach at Harvard University, utilized this sweep to a great extent and with good success. He stated:

> The block on the defensive end is a key block. The right end steps with his near foot driving into the end with a high shoulder block into the numbers. Then he releases to pick up the first man to the inside, who is usually

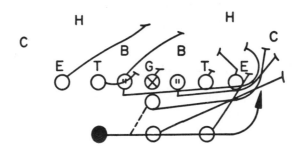

DIAGRAM 3-15

the linebacker. The right tackle blocks the defensive tackle. It is important to stop any penetration by the defensive linemen since we try to clear our guards. The right guard pulls and leads at a minimum depth of two yards. If the end has penetrated, the right guard will drive into him, double teaming with the right halfback. If the guard can clear, he turns the corner and blocks the safety man. The center blocks the man over him. The left guard pulls and leads at a depth of three yards looking to the inside to pick up any pluggers. If he clears, he turns the corner and peels to the inside picking up the first pursuit man. The left tackle, after filling to check the plugger, releases downfield and blocks back. The left end blocks downfield on the safety man. The right halfback drives directly for the defensive end, and using a body block, hooks the end. The fullback only gaining one yard will block out on the corner man using either the shoulder or body block. The quarterback pivots and with two hands pitches a soft dead ball to the left halfback and then leads at over a depth of three yards. He will look to the inside for penetration, turn up the field checking the block on the safety man, and then block the first man to show. The left halfback lead steps gaining a little depth and runs laterally turning up the field behind the quarterback, making his cut according to the blocks in front of him.[2]

Power Sweep Pass

An excellent companion play and closely associated with the end run in Diagram 3-15 is the option run or pass. Both plays support each other. Diagram 3-16 illustrates the same maneuvers as the run, except that the tailback can easily throw the ball. The tight end drives at the defensive end as in the run, but releases sprinting downfield and angles out, usually breaking at ten yards. The right halfback runs at the defensive end, positions himself for a hook block, and then slides out to the flat for approximately five yards. The left halfback takes the ball and prepares to pass. The reaction on the part of the corner man

---

[2] John M. Yovicsin, "Harvard Sweep Series," *Athletic Journal*, Vol. 39, No. 1, 1969, p. 30

will determine whether he will run or pass. If the corner comes up hard, the tailback will throw, and if the corner plays pass, the tailback will run.

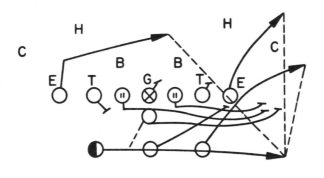

DIAGRAM 3-16
The Option Run or Pass

The Quarterback Sweep Pass and Bootleg

Diagram 3-17 illustrates a Wing "T" with the quarterback throwing the football. In this case, the fullback and tailback block on the line while the wingback and tight end release for a pass. The quarterback can fake the hand-off to the tailback and reverse in the opposite direction for a bootleg (Diagram 3-18) also. In this instance, the quarterback can either hit the split end, tight end, or wingback executing a post pattern. Both guards pull for protection.

DIAGRAM 3-17

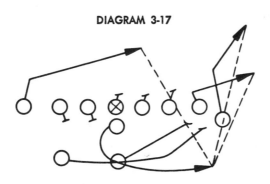

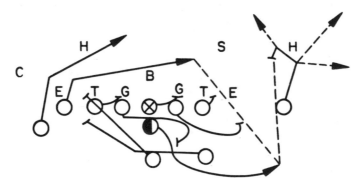

DIAGRAM 3-18

Off-Tackle and Middle Trap

Diagrams 3-19 and 3-20 indicate two excellent trap plays from the off-tackle power play. In Diagram 3-19A the quarterback reverse pivots as normally executed and hands off to the tailback. In this case, however, the first man outside the tackle's nose is to be trapped and the tailback must look and key the block of the pulling guard. The fullback runs for one foot outside the leg of the defender who is being trapped. He influences the man out and blocks on the first man that shows to the outside.

Diagram 3-19B illustrates a similar play except the onside guard pulls and traps the defensive end while the offside guard leads through the hole. The remaining onside linemen block down to the inside. In this case, the fullback goes at the defensive end as if he were to roll block him inside (causing the defensive end to move out) and the onside guard traps him.

DIAGRAM 3-19A
Trapping Off-Tackle

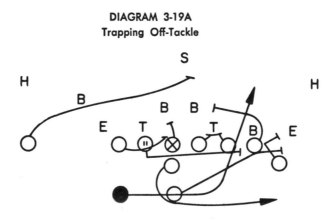

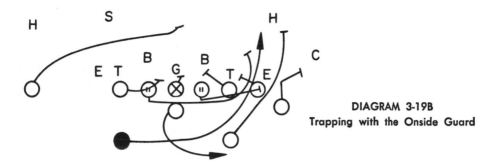

DIAGRAM 3-19B
Trapping with the Onside Guard

A middle trap coming from the off-tackle play is excellent also (Diagram 3-20). The quarterback reverse pivots and hands back to the tailback. The trapper blocks the first man beyond the nose of the center. (Another blocking method is indicated in Diagram 3-21 versus the Split-6 defensive look.)

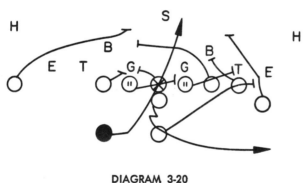

DIAGRAM 3-20
Trapping Up the Middle

DIAGRAM 3-21
Step Around Maneuvers

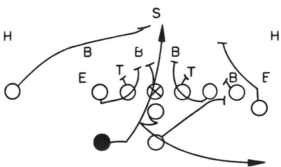

Power Reverse

A *hand-off*-to-*hand-off* reverse is an excellent play versus a great pursuing defense. The play requires much drilling in order to eliminate mistakes and perform the skills necessary. Diagram 3-22 illustrates a fake off-tackle power play utilizing a counteraction by the wingback. The quarterback turns as in the power series, hands off to the tailback and continues downfield. He attempts to get into a position for a lateral. The tailback employs similar techniques in the power sweep, but without slowing down, hands off to the wingback with the inside arm. He then continues as if he is the ballcarrier. The wingback takes one false step, turns, and starts counteraction. He takes an inside hand-off from the tailback and keys the blocks of the pulling guard and end. The offensive end pulls and seals at the hole.

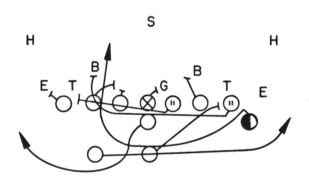

DIAGRAM 3-22

Power Reverse Keep and Bootleg

Play action passes are necessary from almost any good running play. Diagram 3-23 indicates a power reverse bootleg. The quarterback reverse pivots and utilizes the same footwork as in the power reverse. He fakes to the tailback and conceals the ball near his hip while he rolls to the outside. The quarterback can either hit the right tight end releasing on a flag pattern or the left end sprinting to the flat. Another excellent pass from this sequence of plays is to throw back to the tailback swinging downfield. The quarterback can easily pull up and pass the ball to him.

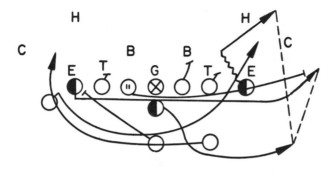

DIAGRAM 3-23

A reverse keep is a good play also (Diagram 3-24). In this instance the quarterback would flow toward the strength. Notice the throwback possibilities to the wingback sprinting downfield.

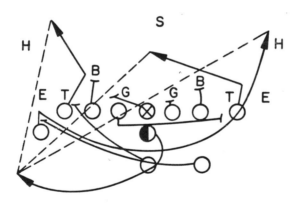

DIAGRAM 3-24

Quarterback Keeper and Flanker Around

Jake Gaither, former Head Football Coach at Florida A & M University, sent the following quarterback power play (Diagram 3-25) away from flow action. He has scored with this sweep in every game. Diagram 3-26 illustrates a flanker-around play he employs also. This reverse gained more than 17 yards per carry for Coach Gaither. The quarterback and setbacks flow one way while the flanker reverses in the opposite direction.

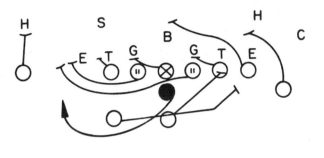

DIAGRAM 3-25

DIAGRAM 3-26

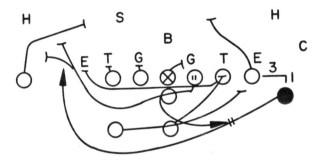

"X" It with the Fullback

A little variation in an offensive play may make or break it. For an example, if the defense is keying and reading backfield maneuvers, their pursuit may stop the offense quickly for no gain. Employing a cross-action within the backfield could help the situation and hold defensive personnel in their positions a little longer. At the same time, however, much power and strength is executed at the desired hole. Diagram 3-27 and 3-28 illustrate the similar sweep and off-tackle power plays as mentioned previously; however, the fullback is driving up the middle attempting to hold pursuit. Similar plays, such as play action passes, bootlegs, and traps, can be utilized with the cross-action of the fullback. A fullback trap is illustrated in Diagram 3-29, with the fullback driving for the middle area.

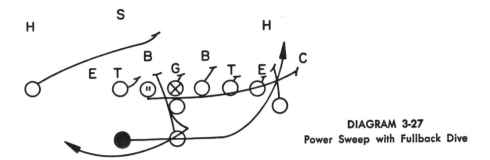

DIAGRAM 3-27
Power Sweep with Fullback Dive

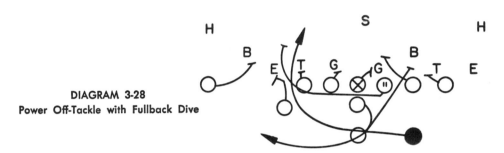

DIAGRAM 3-28
Power Off-Tackle with Fullback Dive

There are a multitude of power plays, with their different formations and variations, throughout the country today. The coach should remember, with a power series, to utilize strength at the hole being attacked. Double-team blocking on either side or both, pulling of guards, tackles and even ends can be done. Employing one, two, or possibly three backs at the hole can be accomplished to add power and strength also. From the power sequence of plays are utilized counters, traps, bootlegs, keepers, reverses, and play action passes in order to use deception versus a defense. The coach must find the formation he desires and form a power series with many variations if he is to win.

DIAGRAM 3-29

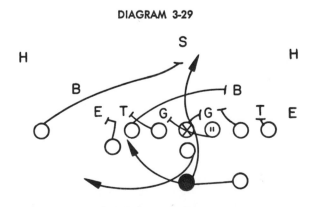

4

The Split T Offensive Series

At Missouri we like to think that the "Split T" is here to stay and that, eventually, it will take its place among the standard formations that have been milestones in the development of football. Its most notable predecessors were the "Bears' T," the "Notre Dame System," the "Warner Single Wing," the "Minnesota System," and the "Short Punt." [1]*

—Don Faurot

Theories and Principles of the Split T Attack

There are five basic theories or principles involved with the Split T attack. The following are the concepts.

1. Maximum speed
2. Straight ahead thrusts over a broad area
3. Faking at the line of scrimmage
4. Utilization of the "best back" principle
5. The principle of average personnel

MAXIMUM SPEED

The design of this type of offense was to hit quickly with great speed at the line of scrimmage. There was no spinning by the quarterback, deep pitches or hand-offs in the backfield. The offensive back did not have to get depth or come forward and then go back from the line of scrimmage.

STRAIGHT AHEAD THRUSTS OVER A BROAD AREA

There are three basic objectives for the offensive line to split in order to widen the defense. The most important objective of the entire Split T attack is to utilize intelligent line splits along the line of scrimmage. By accomplishing

---

[1] Don Faurot, *Football: Secrets of the Split T Formation* (Englewood Cliffs, N.J.: Prentice-Hall, Inc. 1950) p. xiv.

this maneuver the defense must spread. This in turn opens up ready-made holes on the line of scrimmage before the ball is snapped to the quarterback. Diagram 4-1 illustrates a tight offensive line and a split line. With the utilization of wider splits the defense has a much wider area to cover than it does with a tight line. Another important factor is the placement of the offensive backfield. As indicated in Diagram 4-1, the offensive backs are also spread with the line. This gives the backs a greater range and wider area of attack along the line of scrimmage.

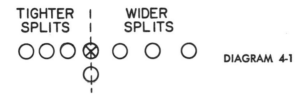

DIAGRAM 4-1

The employment of three offensive backs at their positions in the back-field gives the offense an excellent and balanced area of attack to each side of the offensive center. While the three backs show a good inside offensive punch, the Split T gives the offense an opportunity to get outside quickly and easily.

Another factor in the utilization of a split offensive line is the opportunity to isolate a defensive man on the line of scrimmage. This is done at the hole or the principal point of attack. With the split, and the isolation of the defender, the offensive back has a better opportunity to break into the clear than ever before. The lineman at the attack point must fire-out hard at the defender and take him in either direction. The offensive linemen on either side of the point of attack must contain their defensive counterparts and screen them off from the ballcarrier.

The third objective of splitting the line is: If the defense does not spread and decides to adjust into the gaps created by the splits, the offense can easily block down to the inside and run and pass outside. Diagram 4-2 illustrates a line split and isolating a defender, while Diagram 4-3 indicates the blocking angles on gap defensive linemen (with this the offense can attack outside).

DIAGRAM 4-2

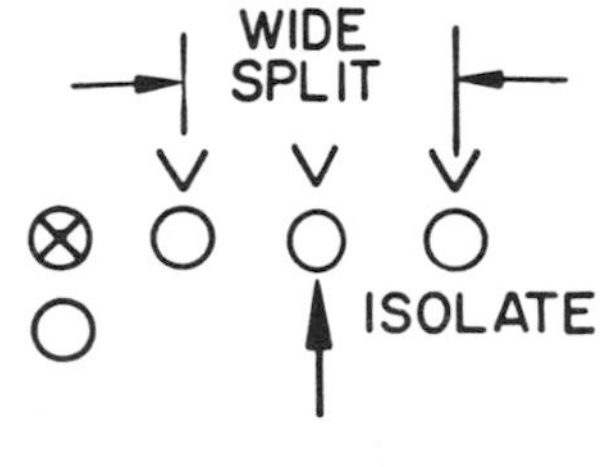

DIAGRAM 4-3

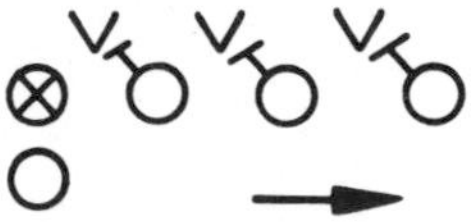

FAKING AT THE LINE OF SCRIMMAGE

In most offensive series, the faking that takes place occurs three to four yards into the backfield. Most faking begins at one point deep in the backfield, and the defense has the opportunity to recover from it and make the tackle easier. This is not the case in the Split T series. Diagram 4-4 clearly indicates

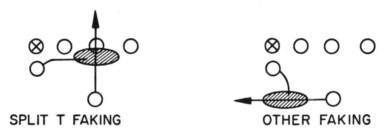

SPLIT T FAKING   OTHER FAKING

DIAGRAM 4-4

the faking areas of the split T attack and the faking required in other attacks. Bud Wilkinson, famous football coach at Oklahoma University, stated in his book *Oklahoma Split T Football:*

> . . . almost all faking occurs at the line of scrimmage. This gives the defense time in which to recover from the fake because the carrying back gains possession of the ball at the line. If we are even momentarily successful with our faking we can materially hurt the defensive team; it will have no time to recover from the fake before we are gaining yardage.[2]

UTILIZATION OF THE BEST BACK

One of the more important ingredients of the Split T attack is quickly getting the best back to the area of attack. As an example, it is the halfback aligned on either side of the offensive center who can most effectively hit the hand-off point from his vantage point. If an offensive halfback from one side

---

[2] Charles "Bud" Wilkinson, *Oklahoma Split T Football* (Englewood Cliffs, N.J.: Prentice-Hall, Inc. 1952), p. 16–17.

of the center must hit the hole on the other side (presume an off-tackle play), the back has a longer time interval in getting to the point of attack. With the Split T attack this does not occur. The halfback nearest the attack area gets to the hole quicker and will either receive the ball from the quarterback or will make a fake into the line. The next ballcarrier (in this case the quarterback) continues down the line to the next hole. In these cases the Split T attack is getting the best offensive back to the area at the quickest possible time. Employed throughout the basic Split T attack, therefore, is the principle of using the best offensive back to attack a certain hole on the line of scrimmage the quickest while utilizing a constant backfield maneuver to either side of the center. Diagram 4-5 shows the plays that can be executed from the Split T attack to either side of the center.

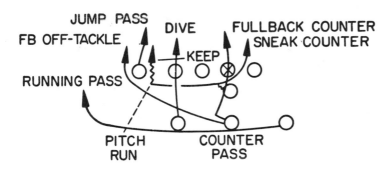

DIAGRAM 4-5

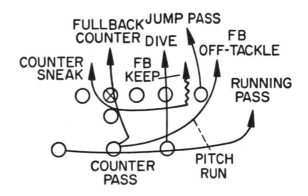

THE PRINCIPLE OF AVERAGE PERSONNEL

Material on a football team will be the difference between winning and losing. One of the reasons Coach Don Faurot decided to attempt the Split T attack was because of the type of personnel he had at hand. While personnel will be discussed further in the chapter, it was felt by numerous coaches that if a coach has average and non-specialized talent on the football team, he could use the Split T attack with success. Any degree of effectiveness would not be lost due to the type of personnel the coach had on the team.

The Strengths of the Split T Attack

The strengths of the Split T sequence of plays are numerous:

1. Splits on the offensive line cause the defense to spread and widen out.
2. The width of the offensive line makes a greater area for the defense to pursue to the ballcarrier.
3. The series requires quick hitting plays along the line of scrimmage. A great deal of speed is utilized.
4. There seldom occurs any loss of yardage due to the speed of the plays and the forward momentum of the offensive backs.
5. The offensive backs can break open into the clear more easily and quickly.
6. It is very simple to learn, teach, understand and know for the ballplayers.
7. Only a few plays are utilized that attack all areas along the offensive line.
8. Players are interchangeable to either side of the line of scrimmage for learning of assignments in case of injury, personnel changes, etc.
9. Offensive faking takes place along the line of scrimmage rather than in the backfield itself.
10. A great deal of deception occurs with the series, because it is difficult (with the quickness and speed) to determine if it is a straight dive, an option, a counter or a pass.
11. The best back in his position hits the hole quickly instead of executing delayed timing.
12. Only average personnel is necessary in a number of positions to make the series successful.

The Formations Most Often Employed

The formation most employed with the Split T attack is the straight "T" formation indicated in Diagram 4-6. It was this formation that gained success for the Split T series.

DIAGRAM 4-6

Of course, other formations can be utilized, but when this is accomplished, much of the attack is taken away. When the formation varies, however, other strengths become apparent. Diagrams 4-7A and B illustrate some of the formations that can be used. Notice that the formations include some type of offensive flanker or split end which widens the defense even more for the passing attack.

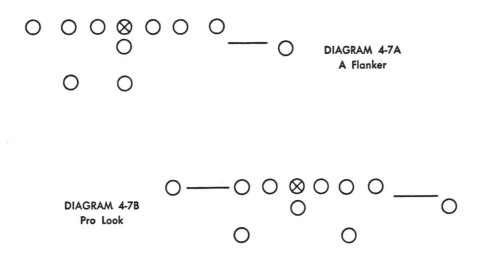

DIAGRAM 4-7A
A Flanker

DIAGRAM 4-7B
Pro Look

Basic Rules for All Plays from the Split T Series

All the plays that will be discussed within the chapter can be blocked very easily. The blocking rules are very simple for the offensive linemen. It must be remembered, however, that some of the rules can be changed if the offensive desires this. This is not necessary from an offensive point of view, but it can be done if the coach wants to change. The following are the offensive line rules for most all players within the Split T sequence. When the plays are illustrated, however, a few minor changes will be indicated to show some of the other methods and techniques that can be employed.

The Tight End:

Outside Running Plays—Block the #3 man inside.
Inside Running Plays—Block the #3 man outside.
Plays away from You—Release inside and block crossfield.

The Tackle:

Outside Running Plays—Block #2 man inside.

Inside Running Plays—Block #2 man outside.

Plays away from You—Release inside and block crossfield.

The Guard:

Outside Running Plays—Block the #1 man inside.

Inside Running Plays—Block the #1 man outside.

Plays away from You—Release inside and block crossfield. For plays over the center, block #1 man.

There are many instances when these simple rules will not hold up versus certain defenses and their adjustments. It is important, therefore, that either different rules be inagurated or line calls be employed on the line of scrimmage so the offense can better cope with the numerous defensive sets. Since there are a multitude of attacks, stunts, blitzes, looks, etc., it is necessary that the offense be able to adjust its blocking patterns to meet these defensive threats.

The Split T Hand-Off Play

The first play that should be developed from the sequence of plays is the straight-ahead dive play. This is illustrated in Diagram 4-8. There are some

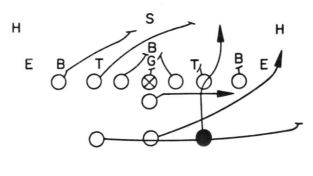

DIAGRAM 4-8

coaches who utilize this as one play, having the dive hit inside, over and outside the offensive tackle. Each play is designated a number so they can be called versus certain defenses. There are other coaches, however, who have the offensive dive man read the defense and cut off the blocks of the offensive linemen. The assignments for the dive play are as follows:

Quarterback

The quarterback receives the ball from the center and steps up and toward the dive man. The step should *never* be back and away from the line of scrimmage. The second step should put him into position to hand the ball off to the dive man. He should hand the ball off with one hand and continue down the line of scrimmage at the defensive end. He should never move backward into the backfield. When he reaches the defensive end, he should fake the pitch or the keep play.

Halfback Ballcarrier

The halfback explodes from his offensive stance and moves straight ahead with all the speed he can muster. When he reaches the line of scrimmage his eyes must be focused straight ahead, not looking for the ball. As he moves toward the line, he should view the blocking on the line of scrimmage. When he receives the ball he can then cut either inside or outside according to the movements of the defensive team. In most cases, the halfback may be cutting back to the inside where his offside offensive linemen are attempting to get in front of him. Diagram 4-9 illustrates another method of blocking on the line of scrimmage. In this case the halfback cuts hard to the inside away from the defensive linebacker.

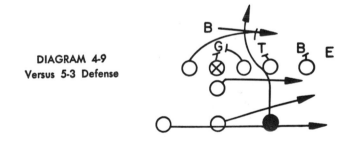

DIAGRAM 4-9
Versus 5-3 Defense

Another method is for the offside offensive guard to employ a pull-around maneuver and block the middle linebacker (Diagram 4-10).

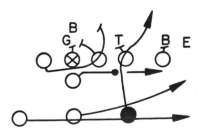

DIAGRAM 4-10

Fullback

On the snap of the ball the fullback takes a crossover step in the direction of the flow and aims for a point two yards in front of the defensive end. He bypasses the defensive end and continues for the defensive halfback as if the play were the quarterback keep or pitch play. If executed correctly, the fullback should maneuver at full speed and block the defensive halfback. This serves two purposes: *One,* the defensive halfback may have a difficult time in determining who has the ball; and *two,* if the ballcarrier cuts to the outside, the fullback's move may be a very important block at that time. The ballcarrier could pitch the ball back to the trailing halfback and the block that is thrown will be very helpful.

Trailing Halfback

On the snap of the ball the halfback should immediately get on the path as if he were to receive the pitch from the quarterback. The halfback, once by the defensive end, should continue downfield to either help block or receive a lateral from the ballcarrier.

Since the blocking rules have already been discussed, Diagrams 4-11 through 4-13 are a few of the defenses with the blocking shown.

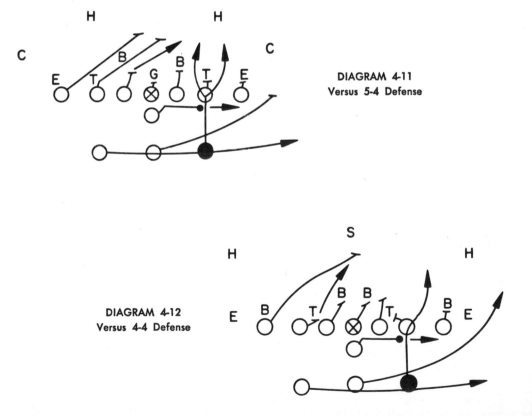

DIAGRAM 4-11
Versus 5-4 Defense

DIAGRAM 4-12
Versus 4-4 Defense

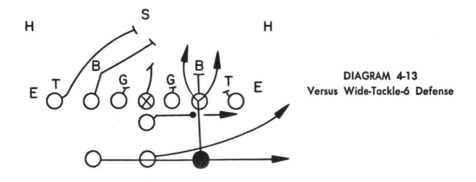

DIAGRAM 4-13
Versus Wide-Tackle-6 Defense

The Split T Option Play

The option quarterback keep or pitch was quite different in the beginning stages than it was in later years. This was noticed by the author as he researched the different books about the subject. As the books became new the play changed. Today, there are numerous methods the coach has at his disposal that he may utilize to have the option play work effectively.

The option play in the beginning was not really an option play at all. It was either a keep with the quarterback running with the ball or a pitch to the trailing halfback. In either case, the fullback was the man who made the block on the defensive end either inside or out and the play would go according to the block by the fullback. Diagrams 4-14 and 4-15 illustrate the pitch and the keep, with the fullback blocking on the corner.

DIAGRAM 4-14
Fullback Blocking Out

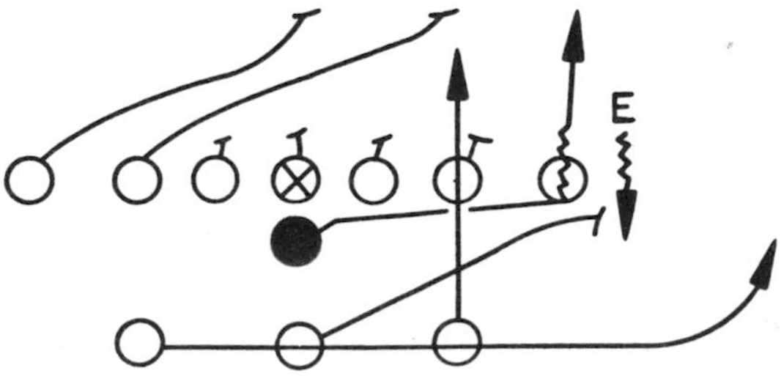

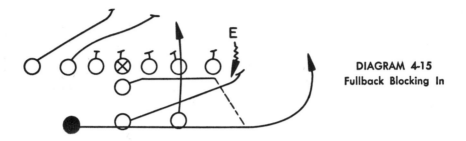

DIAGRAM 4-15
Fullback Blocking In

As time progressed the Split T option, as it is known today, came into existence. The Split T option is illustrated in Diagram 4-16 versus the wide-tackle-6 defense. As can be seen, the fullback goes for the defensive end, but continues on for the defensive halfback. The quarterback comes down the line just as was accomplished in the hand-off play; however, the halfback fakes as if he has the ball. The quarterback comes directly at the defensive end without getting any depth into the backfield. The ball should be kept at chest level. The quarterback should be under control of himself and in a good position to either push off his outside foot and cut upfield or push out the ball with one arm to the trailing halfback.

DIAGRAM 4-16

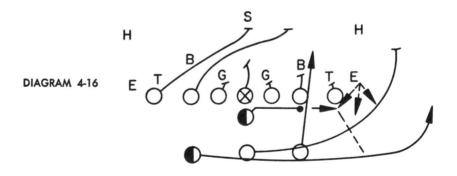

If the defensive end came directly toward the quarterback, he would automatically pitch the ball forward and in front of the trailing halfback. The halfback should be in a position approximately 4 to 4½ yards deep and about two yards in front of the quarterback. This gives the halfback a good chance to break loose and gain some yardage downfield, especially with the fullback blocking on the defensive halfback. The ball must be delivered correctly and never thrown behind the halfback; this slows the running back down and gives the defense an opportunity to pursue him.

If the defensive end does not go for the quarterback, however, he should keep the ball and cut upfield. This is usually the case when the defensive end waits or floats to the outside. Once the quarterback turns upfield, he should attempt to make an outside cut. This is accomplished because the fullback is going for the defensive halfback and the trailing halfback should be cutting up with the quarterback even if he does not receive the pitch. Diagram 4-17 illustrates the quarterback keeping the ball on the option, but then pitching to the trailing halfback downfield.

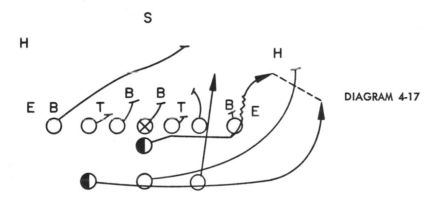

DIAGRAM 4-17

If the number 3 defensive player is hurting the option play, another method that can be utilized is to release the tight end on the defensive secondary and have the quarterback option the #3 man with the fullback blocking the #4 man on the line of scrimmage. This is illustrated in Diagram 4-18 with the offensive tight end blocking ⅓ (or defensive halfback), the fullback blocking on the defensive end, and the quarterback keeping or pitching on the defensive linebacker or #3 man.

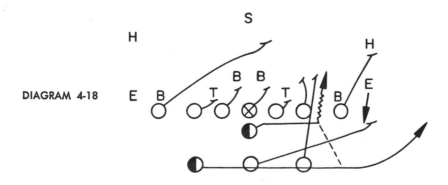

DIAGRAM 4-18

Don Faurot, former head football coach at the University of Missouri, sent the following Split T option (Diagram 4-19) with the employment of a split backfield and a pro formation offensive set. The hand-off, option and pass can easily come off this set. In this case, the flanker causes the defense to adjust. The tight end and flanker release from the line and block the secondary while the quarterback, again, options on the defensive end or #3 man.

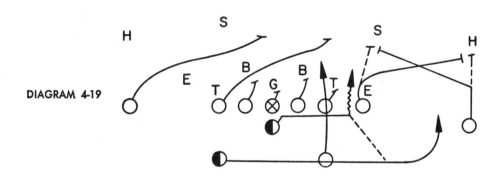

DIAGRAM 4-19

Fullback Off-Tackle Play

A good gainer that can be utilized with the Split T sequence of plays is the fullback off-tackle play (Diagram 4-20). In this case, the entire series begins the same, with the quarterback coming down the line and faking to the diving halfback. The fullback starts out at a forty-five degree angle as before, and when he hits the off-tackle area, he pushes off with his back foot and makes a cut upfield. The defensive end is not blocked. The quarterback hands the ball off and continues at the defensive end.

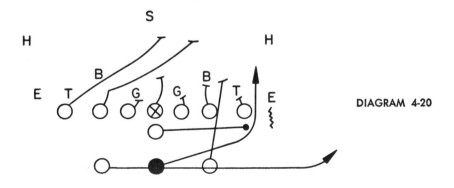

DIAGRAM 4-20

Other blocking maneuvers can be employed at the point of attack. As an example, cross-blocks and traps can be used. Diagram 4-21 indicates the full-back off-tackle play with the onside offensive guard pulling and trapping on the defensive end or number three man. The defensive number four man can be trapped as illustrated in Diagram 4-22.

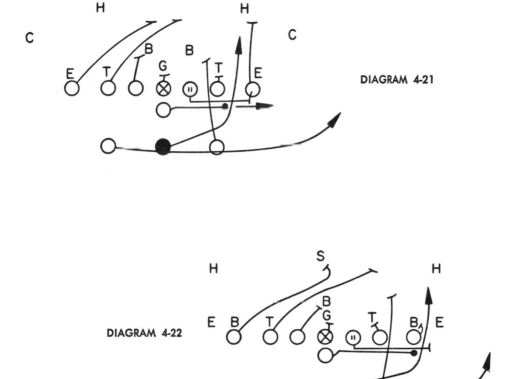

DIAGRAM 4-21

DIAGRAM 4-22

Quarterback Sneak

The quarterback sneak is another excellent play from the Split T series. While the quarterback sneak may be a small intricate play with not much skill involved, it can be one of the most successful plays of the offense. The quarter-back (Diagram 4-23) steps down the line as if to hand the ball off to the dive man. After he takes his first step toward the halfback, he leans in the direction of the dive man as if he is going to hand the ball off. He then pushes off, the first step back toward the center area, and looks for the hole opening. While straight blocking can easily be utilized, other blocking such as cross-blocks, fold blocks and double-teaming can easily be accomplished.

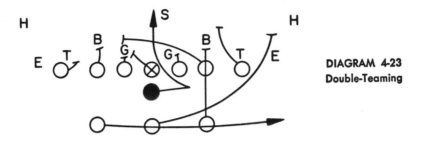

DIAGRAM 4-23
Double-Teaming

The Fullback Counter Play

An excellent play from the Split T is the fullback counter (Diagram 4-24). A big factor is the pursuit of the defensive team. Since the Split T hits quick along the line of scrimmage the defense pursues quickly to the ballcarrier. Counter plays, therefore, are excellent to slow down this pursuit. As indicated in the diagram, the fullback takes a lead step in the direction he usually goes. However, he pushes off one foot and aims for the opposite—or in this case, the left leg of the offensive center. He runs and looks for daylight. Straight-ahead blocking can easily be employed; however, other blocking schemes can be used with a great deal of success. The quarterback takes his first and second step, spins back toward the fullback and hands the ball off. The diving halfback will do all the faking into the line of scrimmage. It is important for the quarterback to remain on the line of scrimmage and not gain depth on his turn back to the fullback.

DIAGRAM 4-24
Fold Blocking Against 5-4

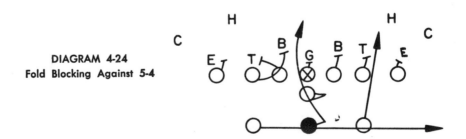

The Split T Counter Option

Diagram 4-25 illustrates a counter type option away from the original flow of the backfield. This can serve as a form of counter play if the defensive team is pursuing well to the front side attack. The blocking on the line of scrimmage is straight-ahead with one-on-one blocking. The onside offensive linemen must hold their blocks due to the delayed timing in the backfield. The quarterback employs the similar steps as in the counter play, but continues down the line of scrimmage for the other defensive end. The fullback must make a good fake up the middle to hold as many defensive linemen and linebackers as possible. In this case, the left halfback uses the same rule as the fullback does on the regular Split T option. The right halfback executes a quick step as if to dive, but reverses his course and becomes the trailing halfback for the pitch. The quarterback utilizes the same techniques and coaching points with the option on the defensive end as he does with the normal option play.

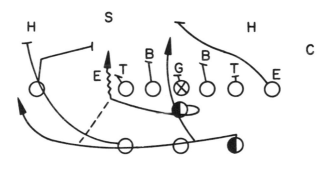

DIAGRAM 4-25

The Split T Trap

Diagram 4-26 indicates a simple trap play that can be used with success. The entire backfield starts in the same direction, but the quarterback hands back to the halfback who is keying the block of the offensive pulling guard. The halfback cuts off the trap block and runs for daylight. The dive back attempts to draw the attention of the defensive man being trapped.

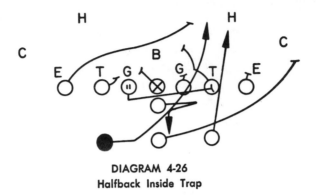

DIAGRAM 4-26
Halfback Inside Trap

Another trap is a quarterback spinner trap (Diagram 4-27). The quarterback comes down the line as was accomplished in the dive. However, the quarterback stops short of the defensive end, makes a complete turn and cuts off the trap block.

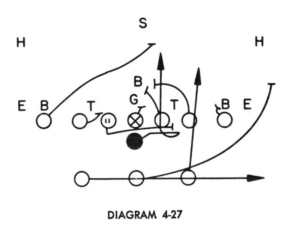

DIAGRAM 4-27

The Split T Reverse

A reverse trap is shown in Diagram 4-28. With this reverse the quarterback comes down the line as if to hand off to the diving halfback. However, the halfback takes one step forward and reverses his steps as illustrated. The fullback and the offside halfback run the same steps and techniques of the Split T option. The onside offensive guard pulls and blocks the first man outside the tackle's block. The quarterback flips the ball back to the reversing halfback who keys the block of the guard and attempts to run off-tackle. In some instances the offside guard could pull and help lead interference. Also, when this occurs, the quarterback must get depth so as not to get in the way of the pulling guard.

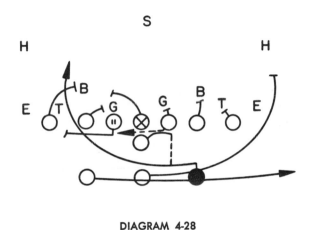

DIAGRAM 4-28

The Jump Pass

The jump pass to one of the tight ends is one of the best pass plays from the Split T series. However, it is not that easy to complete. It is a quick, fast throw that must be very accurate. The play can only succeed if the entire team makes the play look like a run. The offensive linemen must fire-out hard at their defensive opponents, but should not release downfield. The diving halfback must fake as if he has the football. One of the most important aspects of the jump pass is for the diving halfback, once he has reached the line of scrimmage, to make a cut toward the linebacker or linebackers who could interfere with the pass. If he makes a good and proper fake at the line, the linebackers will be somewhat drawn to the dive man.

The offensive end is a vital factor in the success of the play. His pass route will change according to the alignment and play of the defensive linebacker. If the linebacker is stationed to the inside, the end will run outside of him. If the linebacker is outside, the end should go to the inside (Diagram 4-29).

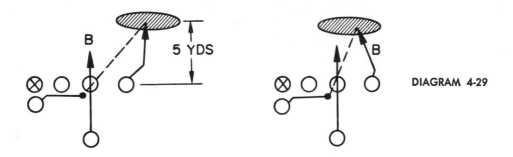

DIAGRAM 4-29

The quarterback's move is important also. He should come down the line as previously mentioned, but should stop short of the diving halfback. He should not go beyond this point because he could be tackled by the defensive man or men outside the offensive tackle. In Diagram 4-29 the proper positioning is vividly shown. Diagram 4-30 illustrates the entire play. Notice, the left end releases to the inside and attempts to block the middle ⅓ or the defensive safety. Once the right end catches the ball, he should look to the inside and cut off this block.

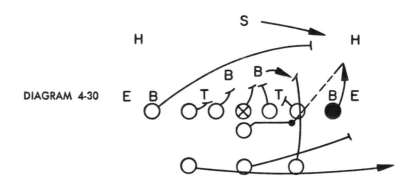

DIAGRAM 4-30

A throwback jump pass can be executed by the quarterback as shown in Diagram 4-31 also. The quarterback maneuvers down the line, stops and throws back to the opposite end. The pass route run will be determined again by the positions of the linebackers and defensive secondary.

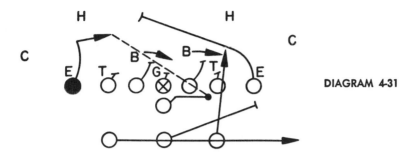

DIAGRAM 4-31

The Running Halfback Pass

One of the first passes to be executed by the Split T sequence of plays was the running pass used by the offensive halfback. Essential to the pass is that the offensive linemen fire-out block, and all the faking in the backfield look exactly like the run. The quarterback comes straight down the line and makes a definite delivery to the halfback. The fullback blocks the defensive end in. The halfback takes the ball and sets for a pass. Any number of pass routes can be utilized with this play. It is important, however, that the halfback be a good passer. This can be drilled enough so the halfback may become very proficient at it. Diagram 4-32 illustrates the running halfback pass where the passer can either hit his offensive end, halfback or opposite tight end. Other pass routes are illustrated in Diagrams 4-33A and B.

DIAGRAM 4-32

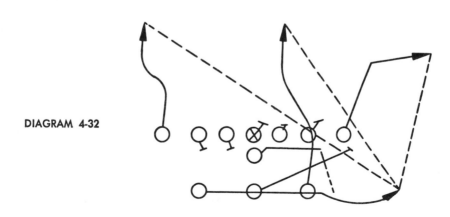

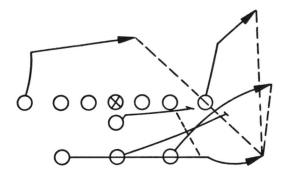

DIAGRAM 4-33A

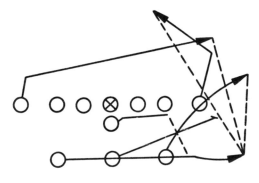

DIAGRAM 4-33B

The Fullback Counter Pass

The fullback counter pass is illustrated in Diagram 4-34. The quarterback does essentially the same techniques as the fullback counter, except that he drops back and looks for an open receiver. In the diagram, the quarterback should look to his right tight end first and then the diving halfback routes

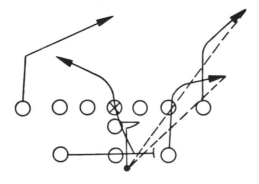

DIAGRAM 4-34

Other Plays from the Split T

Diagrams 4-35 A, B, and C illustrate other plays that can be utilized from the Split T offense. It must be remembered that any number of running plays and passes can be utilized within the series. It is up to the football coach to decipher what he desires to employ and what he does not want to utilize.

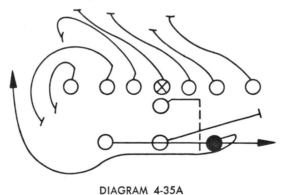

DIAGRAM 4-35A
The Spin Reverse

DIAGRAM 4-35B
The End Around

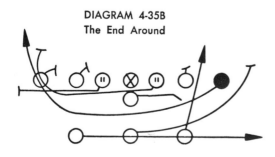

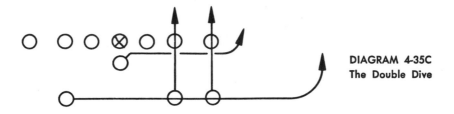

DIAGRAM 4-35C
The Double Dive

The Swing Option

The swing option play came into existence after the Split T had gained great success. Many formations can be utilized with the play. It is excellent both in the middle of the field and going in for a score. Instead of the halfback diving into an area, he swings to the outside and blocks at the corner. Diagram 4-36 illustrates the swing option both from a split and "I" backfields.

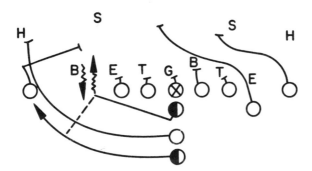

DIAGRAM 4-36

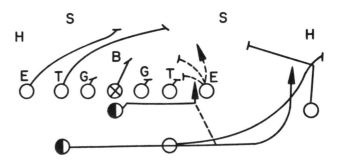

Diagrams 4-37 to 4-39 indicate the Split T option look, but from a three-back "I" look. In the first diagram (4-37) the fake is to the dive man toward the split end side. In the second diagram (4-38) the quarterback fakes to the dive back, reverses his field and options on the opposite defensive end. The fullback swings at the corner and blocks. Motion is indicated in Diagram 4-39 on a swing option with the fullback getting the pitch.

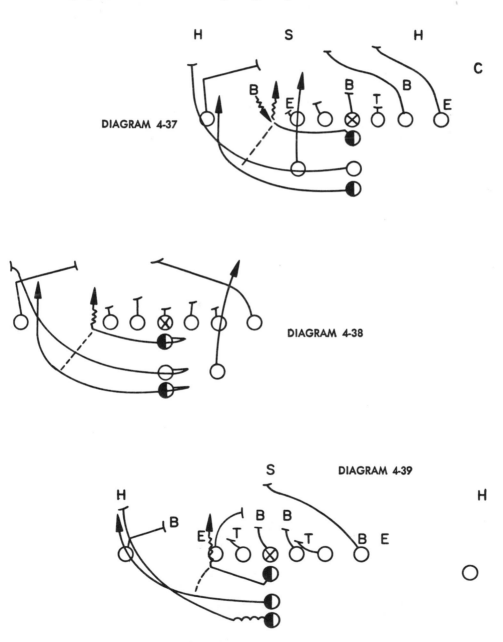

DIAGRAM 4-37

DIAGRAM 4-38

DIAGRAM 4-39

5

The Outside Belly Series

PRINCIPLES AND THEORIES OF THE OUTSIDE BELLY

The theory of the offensive sequence of plays is an attempt to isolate a defensive man, in this case, the defensive end, in order to freeze him at his defensive position not knowing whether the fullback will receive the ball or the quarterback. The play is intended to run off-tackle with good strong blocking inside. Once the defensive man outside the offensive end starts to commit inside, the offense runs and passes outside.

Faking by the quarterback takes place approximately 2½ to 3 yards in the backfield. However, the fake is continuous all the way into the line. If the fullback is handed the ball, he must run hard with his head up, and the quarterback should continue with the fake to the outside. If the quarterback keeps the ball, the fullback should continue into the line of scrimmage and fake downfield to hold the interior defensive people.

The Belly series utilizes the fullback to a large extent. Once the defense has geared itself to these two plays, the other plays within the sequence can be exploited to attack the weak areas of the defense. The play action passes, traps, counters, and reverses can easily be employed if the defense attempts to stop the off-tackle belly play.

The Strengths of the Outside Belly Series

The strengths of the Outside Belly play are as follows:

1. A great deal of faking and deception occur due to the quarterback and fullback's maneuvers.
2. It places the defensive end in a bind as to whether the ball will go inside or outside of his position.
3. It freezes the defensive front alignment as to who is receiving the football.
4. With the deception in the backfield, power occurs at the area of attack, with double-team blocking and other methods employed.

94

5. If the ball is faked off-tackle, the series can exploit around end with an excellent option on the next man outside the number 3 defensive man.
6. Play action passes, reverses, counters, etc., can easily be employed.

Formations to be Utilized

There are numerous formations that can be employed for the Belly series. The most important coaching point to remember is that the fullback should be aligned directly behind the quarterback approximately three-and-a-half to four yards from the line of scrimmage. The Outside Belly began with a basic "T" formation, but other formations developed and the series became more effective. Diagrams 5-1A and 5-1B illustrate two of the formations that can be employed for the Outside Belly sequence of plays.

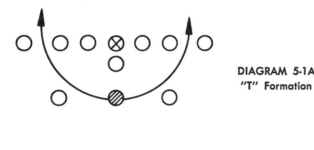

DIAGRAM 5-1A
"T" Formation

DIAGRAM 5-1B
Slot Right Formation

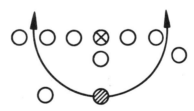

The Play of the Outside Belly

The Outside Belly play has changed and developed since its beginning. However, the basic plays and maneuvers have not altered greatly. Since numerous coaches will use different techniques and fundamentals of the outside belly, an attempt has been made to incorporate all methods here. The coach should utilize his own knowledge, and possibly add to what is stated. Diagram 5-2 indicates the outside belly play. The following are the rules, fundamentals, and techniques.

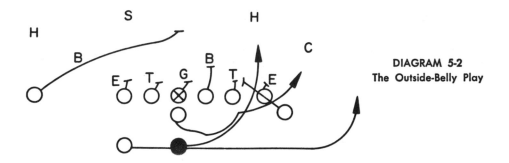

DIAGRAM 5-2
The Outside-Belly Play

OFFENSIVE LINE

Onside End

Rule: Listen for call-block; either block end, linebacker, or double on tackle, etc.

Execution: The onside end will have a number of blocks to perform on the defensive alignment. He may block on a defensive end as in a 5-4, 6-1, or 4-3 defense. Or he could be blocking on a linebacker (4-4 defense) or defensive tackle (Wide-Tackle-6 defense). If he is blocking a defensive end, the offensive end should explode out from his stance directly at the defensive man and execute a face shoulder block. He should aim his head at the mid-section of the opponent and attempt to screen or drive the man off the line of scrimmage. This is one of the most important blocks to be performed.

Coaching Points: Do not lean in the offensive stance. Go directly for the defensive man. Do not go to the ground, but stay with man. Keep the legs driving with short choppy steps, utilizing a wide base.

Onside Tackle

Rule: Make call—block either defensive tackle, on or to inside. If no tackle, look for linebacker.

Execution: The offensive tackle's block is one of the most important blocks in the entire offensive play. If this block succeeds, the play will have a better chance of success. The offensive tackle will perform a number of different blocks according to the defensive alignment and adjustments shown. In many cases, the defensive tackle should be expecting a block from the onside offensive halfback helping to double-team his opponent; however, this will vary. If a defensive tackle is positioned on him, the offensive tackle should fire-out hard and low, attempting to stop any type of penetration. His head should go directly in the middle. If the block is made alone, the tackle's main job is to take the man off the line of scrimmage and attempt to force him inside. If help is received, the head is placed in the middle, sliding to the inside, forcing the legs and butt outside so as to seal any opening that may occur with the block.

Coaching Points: Start with a good offensive stance. Fire-out directly at the man and not to one side or the other. Do not go to the ground. Utilize the hands to keep the body up.

Onside Guard

Rule: Block the number 1 man unless dictated otherwise—double with offensive tackle, step around, or trap.

Execution: Any type of blocking can be utilized on this play. The guard will probably be blocking on a defensive guard, tackle or linebacker. The offensive guard must screen off his defensive opponent as best he can. Since the play is going outside, the guard must work quick to get his man. If blocking on a linebacker, the guard should go for a cut-off point. If he cannot get to him, then attempt to drive the linebacker past the off-tackle hole, hoping the ballcarrier will pick up the block and cut in another direction. If a defensive tackle is stationed over the guard, then the guard should screen the tackle off or scramble block the man. Since the defensive tackle is usually bigger and stronger, he probably will not be able to execute a straight fire-out block on him.

Coaching Points: Explode quick and fast at the defensive man. If trapping, pull quick and block the first man outside offensive tackle's butt. Block inside-out on opponent.

Offensive Center

Rule: Over, front stack, back-gap, linebacker.

Execution: According to the defensive look, the center should strike out hard at his opponent. If a man is stationed head-on, the center should attempt to screen or scramble block him away from the play. If the defensive guard is not quick, however, the center may do well by straight fire-out blocking at the man. If a linebacker is to be blocked, the center should aim for a cut-off point attempting to screen him off. If a front stack exists (Diagram 5-3), the center should stop penetration first and then try to cut the man off.

DIAGRAM 5-3

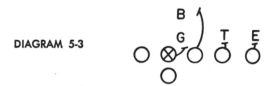

Coaching Points: The center must be quick and fast if he is to block a quick middle guard. He must execute a good center snap to the quarterback first, and then go for the block. Step in the direction of the defensive opponent.

Offside Guard

Rule: Block number 1 man.

Execution: The offside guard must be quick and screen off his defensive counterpart also. If the defensive number 1 man is a linebacker, the guard must move quick attempting to block him. If he cannot block this man, he should drive the defensive linebacker past the hole. This can usually be done if the defensive linebacker is not stepping up into the hole for the ballcarrier (Diagram 5-4).

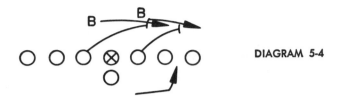

DIAGRAM 5-4

Coaching Points: The offensive guard does not pull on this play. He should put most of his weight forward in order to get a good start at his opponent. However, he should not lean in his stance.

Offside Tackle

Rule: Block defensive number 2 man.

Execution: The offensive tackle should go hard for the defensive man and stay with his block. If the number 2 man is to the inside, he should step down inside and stop any penetration that may occur. (Numerous coaches have the offensive tackle bump the number 2 man and continue downfield and block in the secondary.) The offensive tackle is to screen his opponent from the play.

Coaching Points: The offensive tackle should not take it easy because the play is going away from him. If releasing downfield, release to the inside and go hard. Do not look at ballcarrier because he will cut off the block. Throw block high and near the man. Come up hard looking for other defenders.

Offside End

Rule: Crossfield and chop—block middle ⅓, 3 or 4 deep.

Execution: Release from the line of scrimmage and go for the middle ⅓ of the field. Block the first man that shows in the area. The defensive end could run a pass pattern on this play also. He can fake a pass route and go for the middle area of the field looking for a defensive safety man also.

Coaching Points: When blocking on the safety, the end should look at his opponent to see which way the ballcarrier will make a cut. When the safety makes a cut for the fullback, the end should chop him down.

OFFENSIVE BACKFIELD

Blocking Halfback (Wing)

Rule: Clear the hole.

Execution: On the snap of the ball, the halfback will block according to the blocking scheme utilized by the offensive linemen. He should go directly to the hole area and pick up the first man that shows in the area. There are coaches who do not have the halfback block in the hole, but block outside it. Diagram 5-5 illustrates the onside halfback aiming on the outside shoulder of the defensive number 3 man or end and blocking the first man out from the offensive end. In this case, the halfback will screen his opponent away from the play.

DIAGRAM 5-5

Coaching Points: The halfback should have a good stance. He should go hard for the hole. However, he must remain low and be able to strike hard at the defensive man he is to block. He will either be blocking big defensive ends, linebackers, or tackles. As he makes contact, he should stay low, keep the head up, employ a wide base, and explode hard out at the defender.

Fullback

Execution: From a good offensive stance, the fullback should use a cross-over step first with a lead-step second. His aiming point is the inside leg of the offensive tight end. He should attempt to belly in and square up to the hole as he reaches the line of scrimmage. On about the third step, the quarterback will be placing the ball into the stomach. The fullback should give the quarterback a good pocket for the football. The fullback then squeezes the football and runs for daylight. There are other coaches who have the fullback open-step or lead-step in the direction of the hole. Even other coaches do not have the fullback belly on the play, but have him slant directly to the hole. With these techniques, the quarterback must adjust his maneuvers and steps.

Coaching Points: The fullback should not lean in the direction of the flow. It is necessary for the fullback to be as quick as possible also. Since the fullback is bellying to the hole, the play does become slower. The quicker the fullback, the better the play. The ballcarrier must drive hard up through the hole and then look for running room.

Quarterback

Execution: After getting a good snap from the center, the quarterback should utilize a reverse pivot to approximately 10 o'clock position. The ball should be kept in close to the stomach on this maneuver. He must not stand up high, but should remain low. The next step is directly toward the fullback. The "ride" by the quarterback starts at that point. The quarterback slides one step in the direction of the hole and begins to look at his option man. As the final phase of the slide is executed, the quarterback then continues on for the option man and fakes the belly option play.

Another method for the quarterback to utilize, is to open-step in the direction of the play. The step should be a 45 degree maneuver out and away from the line of scrimmage. He will then take a short second and third step. On the third step, the belly ride begins.

Coaching Points: The quarterback should make his execution perfectly. The ride is short and not long. The fullback and quarterback must work together so the ride becomes effective. The quarterback should not get too shallow or force the fullback deep.

Tailback

Execution: The tailback, on the snap of the ball, will execute a cross-over step, then a lead, and run the chalk line. He should get to a position and fake the belly option pitch with the quarterback. He must remain one-and-a-half yards in front of the quarterback and approximately four yards deep. This is the same position for the option. There are coaches who have the tailback turn upfield instantly, so if the fullback decides to pitch the ball back, the tailback is there to receive it.

Coaching Points: It is necessary to fake the belly option and not take it easy on the play. Do not come forward near the ride of the quarterback and fullback. Stay on the chalk line.

The Belly Option Play

The Belly Option is one of the better offensive plays in football today and probably the best play in the outside belly sequence. The Belly Option is usually executed when the defense starts to tighten down on the off-tackle play. This is especially true with the defensive number 3 man. If he is coming hard for the fullback, the quarterback must call the option.

There are numerous methods to run and block the Belly Option. Many teams will block and double-team the number 3 man on defense and option the next man outside of him. (This is usually a defensive end in an eight-man front or a cornerback in a nine-man defensive look.) There are other methods to utilize also. In some cases, a double-team is not necessary. The onside offensive halfback can release downfield or block on the defensive number 4 man. In this manner, the quarterback can either keep or pitch according to the first defensive man that threatens the play. This will be either the number 4 or 5 (defensive halfback) man on defense.

Diagrams 5-6A and 5-6B illustrate the option play versus an eight and nine man defensive front. The offensive line blocks one-on-one with the defense confronted. Usually the easiest rules are for the offensive linemen to count off from the center *out* and block his man (guard blocks one, tackles takes number two, and the end block the number three man). The offside can either block on their men or release and go downfield.

The quarterback reverse pivots (or steps out according to what the coach desires) and hooks up with the fullback as in the off-tackle play. However, as he completes the ride, the quarterback takes the ball out of the fullback's belly and continues to option on the next defensive number 4 man. As he pulls the ball out, he goes hard for the option man. As he approaches, he must look and react to the movements of this defensive man. If the defender goes for the

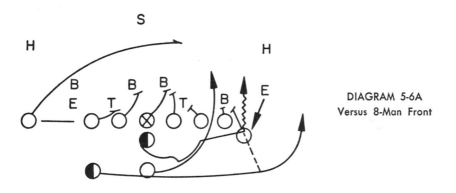

DIAGRAM 5-6A
Versus 8-Man Front

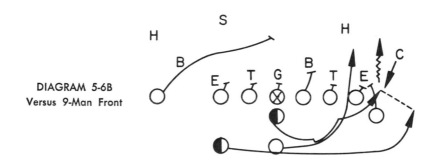

DIAGRAM 5-6B
Versus 9-Man Front

quarterback, he will pitch the football and if he goes for the pitch man, the quarterback will keep the ball and head upfield.

The fullback has an important job in carrying out the fake off-tackle. To execute it correctly, the fullback should continue downfield for approximately ten yards as if he has the football. He attempts to be tackled. The tailback, who receives the football on the pitch, should trail the quarterback as was mentioned in the belly off-tackle play. Once he receives the football, he should run hard and look for daylight. If he does not receive the pitch, he should turn up with the quarterback, in case, at the last second, he decides to pitch the football back. The onside offensive halfback will "clear the hole" (in this case, it is to the outside) and block the first man that shows.

Diagram 5-7A indicates another method, stated previously, with the offensive onside halfback releasing on the defensive number 4 man and blocking in the secondary. Many coaches will not even block the defensive number 3 man—in this case, the end or tackle will release and block in the secondary (Diagram 5-7B).

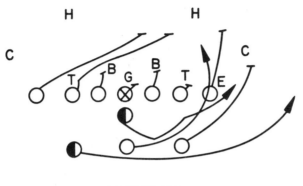

DIAGRAM 5-7A

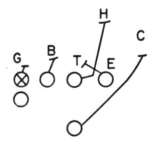

DIAGRAM 5-7B

The Outside Belly Pass

The Outside Belly Pass is very effective in the Outside Belly series. The play begins exactly like the off-tackle play except the quarterback pulls the ball out of the fullback's belly, steps a little deeper than the option, and throws the ball on the run. He attempts to get outside the defensive end on the line of scrimmage. The fullback should carry out the same fake. The tailback similarly begins as in the option, but comes up quick and blocks the first man outside the offensive end. He should attempt to get his head on this man's outside knee and roll block the defensive end. The quarterback steps behind the tailback's block and attempts to get outside.

The onside offensive end will block one count and release into the flat area approximately 5 yards in depth. The wingback will release immediately and run a flag pattern. If there is no wing, but an onside halfback, the offensive end and halfback can change assignments, with the end running flag and the halfback going to the flat. The offside end will release and trail approximately 8 to 10 yards in depth. The onside offensive linemen should fire out at their defensive counterparts and make the play look like a run. The offside linemen can execute cup block techniques. Diagram 5-8 illustrates the belly option pass.

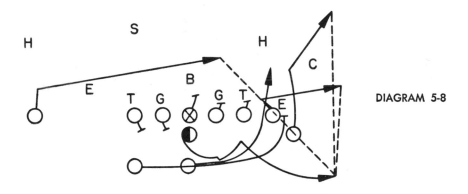

DIAGRAM 5-8

The Outside Belly Trap

The Outside Belly Trap is a good play, especially when the defense is over-pursuing both the outside belly off-tackle and the option. It is also excellent if the interior linemen or tackle is reacting quick to the outside. The entire play starts as if the off-tackle play were to be run. However, the quarterback, after riding the fullback, hands back to the tailback. The ballcarrier employs a cross-over step technique, but on the second lead-step he cuts up hard, reading the pulling guard's block. The offensive linemen utilize normal trap rules versus the defenses and their adjustments (Diagram 5-9).

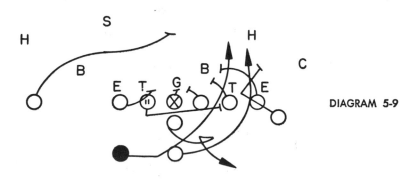

DIAGRAM 5-9

The Inside Reverse

Diagram 5-10 illustrates an inside reverse from the off-tackle play. In this case, the wingback comes inside the belly ride fake of the quarterback and fullback. He will take an inside hand-off from the quarterback. The offensive linemen can block this a number of ways. Trap blocking can be utilized. Another method is for the offside linemen to cup block as if it were a play action pass. On approximately the second count, the offensive guard and tackle will strike at the defensive men with a fire-out block technique. The wingback, after receiving the ball, will look for daylight. The onside linemen will block as if it were an off-tackle play. The fullback will continue to fake downfield.

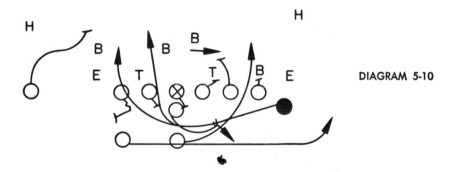

DIAGRAM 5-10

The Outside Reverse

The outside reverse (Diagram 5-11) is an excellent play if the defensive team has a great deal of pursuit once the ball goes in one direction. It is good when the defensive secondary away from the flow goes quickly on rotation or pursuit also. In many cases, the reverse to the outside will gain good yardage

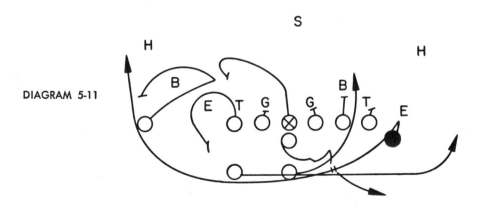

DIAGRAM 5-11

especially when the defense least expects it. The execution for the offensive back-field is rather simple. However, the offensive linemen must put in a tremendous amount of time in order to block defenses correctly.

The quarterback, fullback, and tailback execute the belly off-tackle play. The wingback will take one jab step to the outside, will pivot to the inside and go deeper than the quarterback-fullback ride. He will take an outside hand-off from the quarterback. The onside end (the end to where the play is running) will release downfield as if the play were going in the opposite direction. At approximately 5 to 6 yards, he will cut outside and come back on either inside pursuit such as linebackers, or block on defensive secondary men. The onside tackle blocks straight ahead, hoping his defensive opponent will go into pursuit. Penetration cannot be made by this defensive man. After the technique has been performed, the tackle will roll around and come back on the defensive end. The tackle must react quickly and get to a position approximately one yard behind and two yards outside the defensive end. When the chasing defensive end notices the reverse, he will start to turn, and this is the instant the offensive tackle should execute the block. The offensive guard will hit out in front of him to prevent any penetration. He will then head for the flat area and block in that ¼ of the field. The offensive center hits his man and peels back on any inside pursuit by the defensive front men and stay with their opponents as if the play were a run to their side.

The Roll-Back Pass

An excellent pass from the belly is the roll-back play action pass shown in Diagram 5-12. The quarterback executes the ride with the fullback, pulls the ball out, and aligns behind the offensive center approximately 7 to 8 yards in depth. Any number of patterns can be used with the offensive receivers.

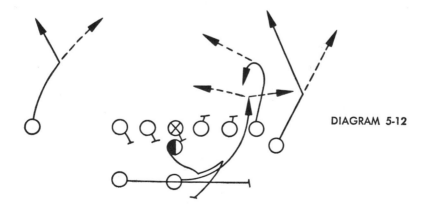

DIAGRAM 5-12

The Inside Reverse Pass

Diagram 5-13 indicates the inside reverse pass. The quarterback and the entire backfield execute the inside counter play. The quarterback initiates a good fake to the wingback, delays for a split second, and attempts to get outside the defensive end. The tailback blocks exactly as if the play were the outside belly pass. The fullback runs to the flat. Another play pass is for the quarterback to pull up and throw back to the wingback sprinting downfield (Diagram 5-14). Any pass route could be executed.

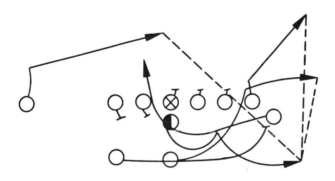

DIAGRAM 5-13

DIAGRAM 5-14

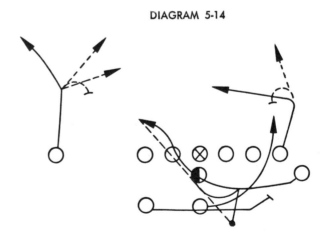

6

The Inside Belly Series

Attacking the Middle First

There are not many play sequences that begin with the base play attacking the middle area first. Most sequences of plays enjoy attacking either outside or off-tackle first and then running or passing at other areas of the defense. The inside belly series attacks directly up the middle of the defensive front alignment. It attempts to put pressure at the middle defensive people. Therefore, the defense must concentrate to stop the quick pop up the middle. The sequence of plays can easily attack other areas of the defense quickly and easily if the defense attempts and accomplishes this.

Theory and Principle of the Inside Belly Series

The theory of the Inside Belly sequence of plays is an attempt to isolate a defensive man, namely the defender aligned over or near the offensive guard. The offense hopes to hold or freeze this man so he will not know who is receiving the football. If the fullback can put enough pressure on the middle defenders to isolate them in their positions, the other plays should gain and have good success.

The Strengths of the Inside Belly Series

There are many strengths to the Inside Belly series. The following are some of the points to remember.
1. A great deal of faking and deception occurs due to the quarterback's and fullback's maneuvers.
2. While faking and deception are taking place, an abundance of power is utilized with the fullback. Power blocking can easily be utilized at the point of attack also.

3. The middle defender or defenders are put into a bind as to whether the ball is coming at them or going to the outside.
4. The defensive front alignment must stay at their positions until they know who is receiving the football.
5. The backside defensive alignment cannot go quickly on pursuit, because they must hold for counters and reverse plays.
6. If the ball is faked over the middle area, the quarterback can hand the ball off to the tailback or can run with the ball himself.
7. Play action passes, reverses and different counters can easily be utilized in the offensive series.

THE PLAY OF THE INSIDE FULLBACK BELLY

The fullback Inside Belly is, at certain instances, the fullback drive, slant, or buck play. This is the starting point for the entire sequence of plays. The offense hopes to drive the fullback up the middle area and cause the defense to tighten and keep them conscious of the fullback. Once this has been accomplished, the Inside Belly series, with all of its plays, will execute and run easier. In most cases, the defense will attempt to stop the fullback buck, due to the fact it is the primary play of the series. However, the offense must run this so other plays will execute better. The fullback belly may not gain as the other plays within the sequence, but it helps the other plays enjoy success.

Once the defense starts to commit in the middle area and the defensive tackles begin to stop the play, the offense can attack off-tackle and outside. With the fullback driving hard up the middle, it is difficult for the play to lose any yardage. The offensive line should fire-out hard and tough while the fullback must look for daylight. Diagram 6-1 illustrates the Inside Belly play versus the 5-4 Oklahoma defense. The rules, executions and coaching points of all positions follow.

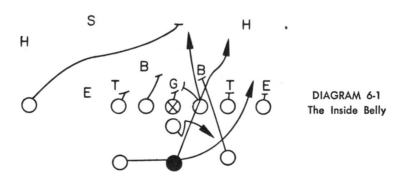

DIAGRAM 6-1
The Inside Belly

OFFENSIVE LINE

Onside End

Rule: Block number 3 man unless indicated otherwise.

Execution: On the snap of the football, the end drives out hard for the defensive number 3 man and executes a good fire-out drive block. He should screen the defensive opponent to the outside. He aims the head at the mid-section of the defensive man and drives him off the line of scrimmage.

Coaching Points: He goes directly for the defensive man. He should make the play look as if the ball-carrier were going to run off-tackle. He must not go to the ground, but he should stay with the man. He keeps the legs driving with short driving steps utilizing a wide base.

Variation: The offensive end can release from the line of scrimmage as if the play were to be a play action pass. He will go downfield, however, and block on the defensive secondary. This will hold the secondary defenders from coming up hard to stop the momentum of the offensive fullback. He should throw a downfield block on the defender and chop him down.

Onside Tackle

Rule: Block number 2 man unless indicated otherwise by call.

Execution: The offensive tackle blocks his man by putting his head into the middle of his defensive counterpart. If blocking straight ahead, the tackle should attempt to drive the defensive man outside. Since the play is going to the inside, the tackle should utilize an inside-out block. It is important for the tackle to keep his legs underneath him in the hole being run. Attempt to drive the man off the line of scrimmage.

Coaching Points: The tackle should explode out hard at the defensive counterpart. Keep the legs driving and do not go to the ground. If the defensive man is in gap, he should not allow penetration. Put the head across and drive the man down the line. If blocking the linebacker, drive out hard and do not lose contact.

Onside Guard

Rule: Block number 1 man unless call indicates otherwise.

Execution: The offensive guard's block is one of the most important blocks in the entire offensive play. If this block succeeds, the fullback play will probably have a great deal of success. The fullback is driving up over the guard and it is, therefore, important that the guard do the best job possible. The offensive guard will have to perform a number of different blocks according to the type of defense and adjustment seen. The defensive man may be directly over him, in the inside gap, outside gap, in a linebacker position, etc. If a defensive guard is stationed over him, the offensive guard should fire-out hard and low attempting to stop any penetration and drive the defender back off the line of scrimmage. His head should go directly in the middle. He should drive the man straight ahead; the fullback will break to either side of the block.

Coaching Points: He should not lean in the offensive stance. Fire-out directly at the defensive man. He should not take a circled path to get at defender. The tackle cannot go to the ground. He should employ the hands to keep the body off the ground and in good control.

Center

Rule: Block number 0 man, front stack, back gap, off-side linebacker.

Execution: According to the defense that is set up, the offensive center should strike out hard at the defender. If a man is positioned over him, the center must drive this man away from the hole. The center is probably the next most important man for the inside fullback belly to be successful. The head should go directly for the mid-section and slide to either side according to where the ball is being run. The arms must come up and the feet must drive hard. The center must not lose his block on this play. If possible, screen the defensive man from the hole. If a front stack exists, the center should stop any type of penetration, but may need help from the onside guard.

Coaching Points: A proper snap and good exchange must be made with the quarterback. Step directly to the defensive man being blocked. Stay low, hit hard and come up through the man. Keep a wide base and use short driving steps to accomplish the job.

Offside Guard

Rule: Block number 1 man.

Execution: On the snap of the ball, the offside guard should move quick and execute a good block on his defensive man. If the defensive number one man is a linebacker, the offensive guard must move quick to cut the man off from the play. Attempt to screen the defensive man from the area being attacked. Stay with the defender as long as possible. Keep the feet moving and try to tie the defensive man up.

Coaching Points: The guard should not lean in the stance. Weight can be forward due to the fact no pulling is necessary. Move quick and fast. Keep head up, stay low, employ a wide base and do not go to the ground.

Offside Tackle

Rule: Block number 2 man.

Execution: The offensive tackle should go hard for the defensive number 2 man and stay with his block. If a man is to the inside, the tackle should step hard to the inside and prevent any penetration. If the man is stationed over, the offensive tackle should screen this man away from the play and prevent any type of pursuit.

Coaching Points: The offensive tackle should not go to the ground. Keep the body up and keep contact with the defensive man. Do not take it easy on this play even though ball is going away, because the defenders may make the tackle.

Offside End

Rule: Crossfield and chop—block middle ⅓, 3 or 4 deep.

Execution: The end should release from the line of scrimmage and go for the middle ⅓ of the field. He should block the first man that shows in the area. The offensive end could run a pass route on the inside belly play. He can fake a pass route and then go for the middle area of the field for a defensive safety man also.

Coaching Points: The end should not look at the ballcarrier; the ballcarrier will cut off the block. Look at the defensive man to be blocked and see which way the fullback is to cut. Once the secondary man makes his move, chop him down.

OFFENSIVE BACKFIELD

Blocking Halfback (Wingback)

Rule: Clear the hole—unless indicated otherwise.

Execution: On the snap of the ball, the halfback will block according to the blocking scheme employed by the offensive linemen. In many cases, the halfback will not have to be used up the middle area. He can be employed at other areas to help faking, etc. Diagram 6-2 illustrates the halfback blocking away from the area being attacked. When clearing the hole, however, he should go directly up and through the hole area and pick up the first man showing in the area. Usually the back will recognize the defense and know who to block.

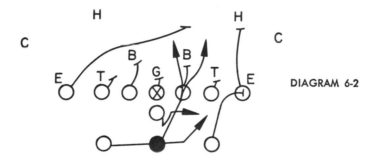

DIAGRAM 6-2

Coaching Points: Come in hard and low at the defender. The defensive man may be tough to root out and it is important to put the head in the middle and drive up and through opponent. Keep a wide base and utilize hard driving steps.

Fullback

Execution: From a good offensive stance, the fullback should run directly at a point over the offensive guard. His first step is a lead step in that direction. He remains low with his head up. His inside elbow and arm come up right away to receive the ball from the quarterback. The fullback should drive hard and fast for the offensive guard and run for daylight. He should not run with his head down.

Coaching Points: The fullback should not circle his path, but should run on a straight line to his aiming point. The quicker the fullback gets to the hole, the better it will be. He should not attempt to go slow on this play. Once he receives the football he must tuck the ball away hard, because he will be hit many times from the defensive front alignment.

Quarterback

Execution: From a good offensive stance, the quarterback takes a direct snap from the center and open-steps back directly for the fullback. It is important the step be back and not down the line. This may prevent a good exchange with the fullback. As he steps he places the ball into the pocket of the fullback. He rides with the fullback into the line, but does not go beyond his (quarterback's) belly. In this case, the quarterback steps with his right foot, slides up with his left and continues down the line of scrimmage as if he has the football. His next fake is with the offensive tailback who is running at the off-tackle hole. After he fakes to the tailback, he continues to the outside faking the quarterback keep play.

Coaching Points: The quarterback should place the football into the pocket of the fullback with two hands. He should not reach out with the fullback, but must mesh with him at a close distance. The quarterback should not be high, nor low to the ground.

Variation: There are many coaches who teach their quarterback to reverse pivot instead of an open-step in the direction of the play. When reverse pivoting, the quarterback must move very quickly and cannot get into the running lane of the fullback. The reverse pivot is almost a spinning maneuver directly at his quarterback position. Usually a reverse pivot is employed by coaches, because it will coincide with the reverse pivot utilized by numerous coaches in the outside belly series.

Tailback

Execution: On the snap of the ball the tailback should execute a crossover lead step in the direction of the play. On the second or lead step, the tailback should start to aim and direct his steps at the off-tackle area. His steps and maneuvers should coincide with the movements of the fullback's and quarterback's. On the third step the tailback must bring up his inside arm to fake the hand-off with the quarterback. Once the fake has been made, the tailback should run hard for the off-tackle hole and continue running as if he has the ball.

Coaching Points: The tailback must not lean in his offensive stance. It is important for the tailback to run hard on this play and not take it easy. He must make it look as if he is receiving the football and running off-tackle. He should not come forward too quickly to lose the faking between the quarterback and himself.

The Off-Tackle Run

The off-tackle belly is probably the next most important play for the inside belly sequence of plays (Diagram 6-3). When the defensive tackle, or front alignment, is jamming the middle to halt the fullback, the quarterback should

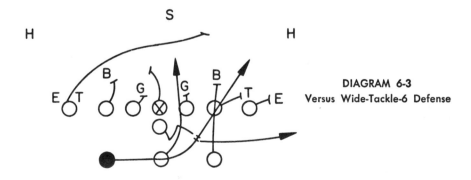

DIAGRAM 6-3
Versus Wide-Tackle-6 Defense

call the off-tackle play. It is a hard-hitting maneuver where deception on part of the offensive backfield is important.

Diagrams 6-4A to 6-4D illustrate other blocking that can be utilized versus numerous defenses. It is important that the fullback drive hard for the middle

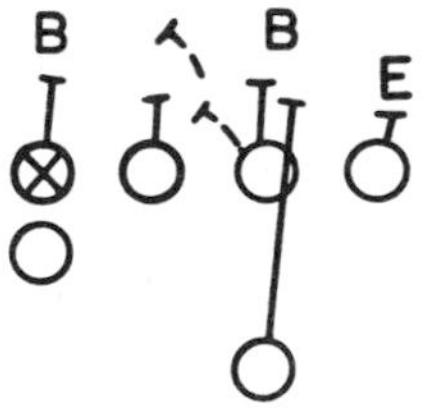

DIAGRAM 6-4A
Versus 4-3 Defense

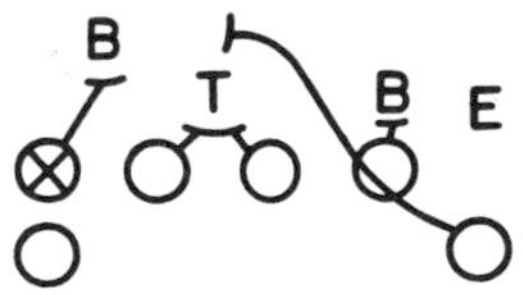

DIAGRAM 6-4B
Versus 4-4 Defense

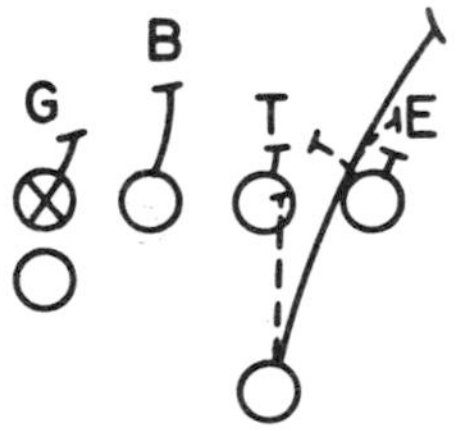

DIAGRAM 6-4C
Versus the 5-4 Defense
(Cross-Block)

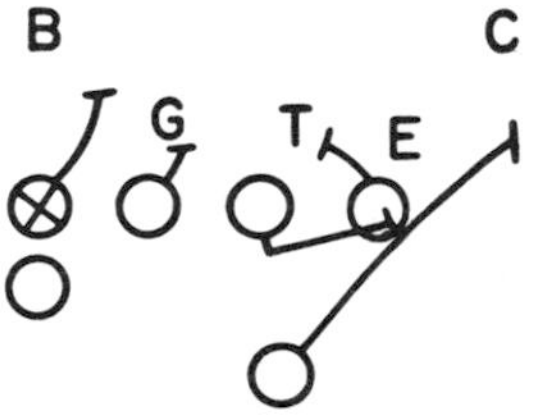

DIAGRAM 6-4D
Versus 6-1 Defense
(Straight, Double Tackle, etc.)

area as if he is receiving the football. He cannot take it easy and slow down. He must execute a good fake so he will be tackled by the front middle defenders. The quarterback employs similar techniques with the fullback as was described previously. Once the ride has been accomplished, however, the quarterback pulls the ball out from the fullback and steps at approximately a 45 degree angle away from the line of scrimmage. He hands the ball off to the tailback approximately 1½ to 2 yards off the line of scrimmage. In this instance, the tailback runs hard for the hole, keeps his head up and runs for daylight. Any combination of blocking with the offensive linemen and onside offensive back can easily be accomplished.

Off-Tackle Quarterback Keep

The quarterback keep play off-tackle is an excellent variation to the tailback run. Diagram 6-5 indicates the quarterback faking to the fullback, then tailback and keeping the ball. He follows the tailback up through the hole. The tailback fakes as if he has the football and then helps to block in the area.

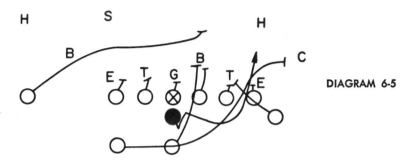

DIAGRAM 6-5

Quickie Pass to Tight End

An excellent play action pass (Diagram 6-6) can be utilized from the fake of the fullback dive. The quarterback will execute the same techniques and maneuvers as with the fullback dive, except he will pull the ball out of the pocket and look for the tight end breaking downfield. The tight end's course is straight downfield, and he should not veer to the inside so the line-backers will not interfere with the pass. The fullback should drive hard as if he has the ball to force the defensive front people to come at him. The offensive linemen must fire-out block so not to give the play away as a play action pass.

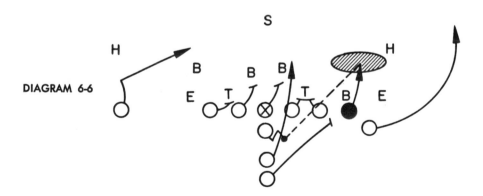

DIAGRAM 6-6

Once this play has been executed a few times, the quarterback could fake to the fullback, fake the pass to the tight end and drop back to hit the wingback or onside halfback running down the sidelines (Diagram 6-7). The quarterback could also throw back on this play to another receiver.

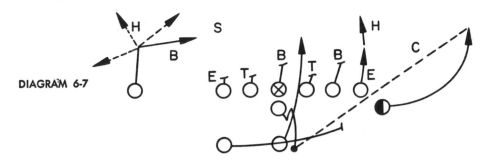

DIAGRAM 6-7

The throw-back quickie pass to the offside end is indicated in Diagram 6-8. In this case, the quarterback fakes to the fullback and looks to the offside end in an open area. It is important for the end to run for a clearing in the defensive secondary away from the inside linebackers.

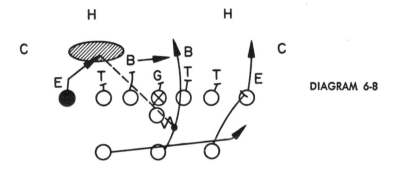

DIAGRAM 6-8

The Quarterback Keeper

Once the defensive front alignment begins to jam inside attempting to stop both the fullback drive and the tailback off-tackle, the quarterback keeper must be called (Diagram 6-9). The quarterback fakes to the fullback, tailback, and keeps the ball by running outside around end. This play should not be called unless the defensive end is continually coming hard down to the inside trying to stop the inside or the off-tackle play. The keeper can then be executed.

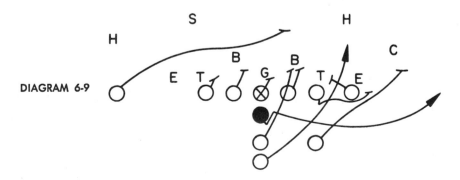

DIAGRAM 6-9

The Inside Belly Option

It is difficult to run an option play from the formations illustrated up to this point. Usually the blocker must be eliminated, but used as the running back or the option man. Diagram 6-10 illustrates the 3-back "I" formation versus a 5-3 defensive front. As can be seen, there is no blocker to the tight end side. The quarterback open-steps, fakes to the fullback, then tailback, and keeps the ball as in the quarterback keeper outside. However, the quarterback has a trailing halfback who he can utilize versus the next defensive opponent that shows. This is usually the number 4 man. If the defensive man comes for the quarterback, the quarterback will pitch the ball to the trailing tailback. If the defensive man goes for the halfback, the quarterback will keep the football and turn upfield. The trailing halfback should turn upfield behind him also in case the quarterback decides to deliver the ball back.

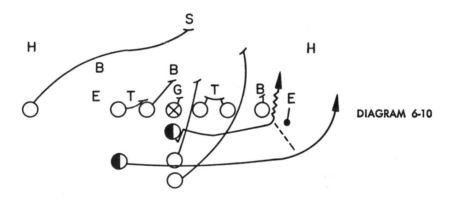

DIAGRAM 6-10

The Off-Tackle Play Action Pass

Diagram 6-11 illustrates the play action pass from the off-tackle tailback run. The wingback releases from the line and runs a flag route. The tight end blocks for two counts on the defensive number 3 man and releases for the flat area. The offside end will come across the field on a trailing pattern. The offensive line block straight ahead as if it is a run. The backside can utilize cup blocking. It is most important that the fullback and tailback execute good fakes up the middle and off-tackle to hold the defensive men to their positions. The quarterback fakes to both the fullback and tailback and continues outside to either run or pass the football. If a receiver is open, he should pass the ball to him. If there is any running room, however, the quarterback should attempt to run the football. The tailback must execute a good fake to hold the defensive end or number 3 man.

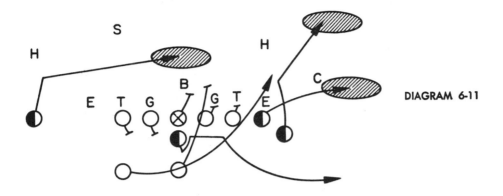

DIAGRAM 6-11

Hand-Back Counter

Counters are important in this series, especially when the defense is pursuing quickly to the fullback and tailback. The hand-back counter is an excellent play for the middle area (Diagram 6-12). The quarterback fakes to the fullback and reverses back to hand-off to the tailback running hard through the middle area. Blocking can be straight ahead, or step-around maneuvers can be used.

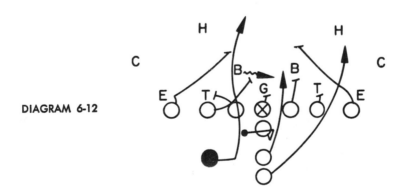

DIAGRAM 6-12

The Counter Option

The counter option play from the hand-back counter is indicated in Diagram 6-13. The quarterback fakes to the fullback, then fakes to the tailback coming up the middle and continues down the line at the defensive number 3 man. If the defender comes for the quarterback, the quarterback will pitch the football to the trailing halfback. If the defense man goes for the halfback, the quarterback will keep the football.

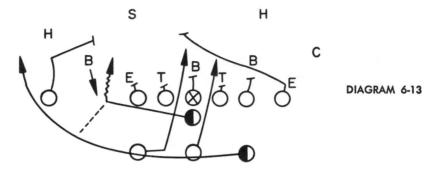

DIAGRAM 6-13

The Hand-Back Counter Pass

Diagram 6-14 illustrates the play action pass from the hand-back counter. After the quarterback fakes to the diving tailback, he will retreat back and hit any receiver who is open. Any number of pass patterns can be installed with the backfield maneuver utilized.

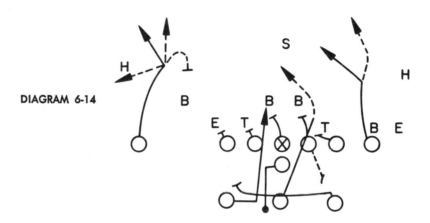

DIAGRAM 6-14

The Inside Counter

Another counter is shown in Diagram 6-15. On this play, the quarterback executes maneuvers with the fullback similar to the inside belly, except he does not go into the line. The halfback, on the side of the play, takes a step into the line with his outside foot, then pivots on this foot and initiates his next step toward the center area with the inside foot. He coordinates his steps with maneuvers and movements of the quarterback and diving fullback. The quarterback initiates a front hand-off with the halfback. The halfback runs for the middle of the line looking for any daylight. Blocking on the line of scrimmage can differ from straight-ahead, cross-blocking, to step-around maneuvers. A variation of the play is the quarterback can ride with the fullback into the line of scrimmage and execute a back hand-off to the tailback.

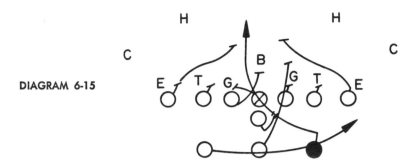

DIAGRAM 6-15

The Quarterback Counter

A simple play, but one which can gain a good deal of yardage, is the quarterback counter (Diagram 6-16). The quarterback utilizes techniques similar to the inside fullback belly play. However, once the ride has been executed, his weight should be on the forward foot. The quarterback will spin on this foot and reverse pivot to the other side of the offensive center. He will hold onto the football and run for daylight. Some teams and coaches do not utilize a reverse pivot on the forward foot, but advocate the quarterback shorten the stride of the ride and go directly for the offensive center and run with the ball. Usually straight-ahead blocking is employed; however, cross-blocks and step-around maneuvers can be utilized.

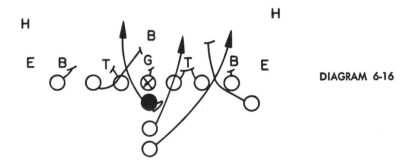

DIAGRAM 6-16

The Fullback Trap

The fullback drive play can be trapped also (Diagram 6-17). In this case, the quarterback hands the ball off as he does in the inside fullback belly. The offside guard pulls and blocks the first defensive linemen past the nose of the offensive center. The fullback reads the block of the guard and looks for daylight. The same assignments for the backfield are used as accomplished with the inside fullback belly play.

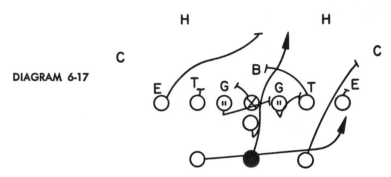

DIAGRAM 6-17

The Inside and Outside Reverse

Diagram 6-18 illustrates the inside reverse. The quarterback executes a hand-off to the halfback after riding the fullback into the line. The offside guard pulls and leads for the ballcarrier. The fullback plugs the hole for any defensive penetration.

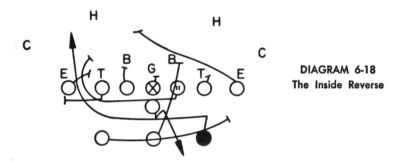

DIAGRAM 6-18
The Inside Reverse

Diagram 6-19 shows the outside reverse from a wing formation. In this case, the quarterback fakes to both the fullback and tailback before handing the football to the wingback. The ballcarrier jab steps before going in the opposite direction of the flow. The onside tight end peels back for the defensive end while the onside tackle blocks, stopping penetration and goes to the flat area looking for any off-color jersey. The offside guard can pull and lead interference also.

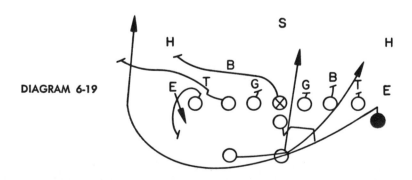

DIAGRAM 6-19

The End-Around Play

Diagram 6-20 illustrates an end-around play versus a wide Tackle-6 defense. This is an excellent maneuver, because the defense cannot obtain a key from any of the backfield actions. The entire backfield is flowing in one direction while an offensive lineman (tight end) becomes the ballcarrier. The quarterback rides the fullback into the line and hands back to the tight end. The left and right halfbacks go with the flow of the belly action. The offside guard pulls and traps the defensive end. The tight end takes the football from the quarterback and reads the block of the guard. He runs for daylight.

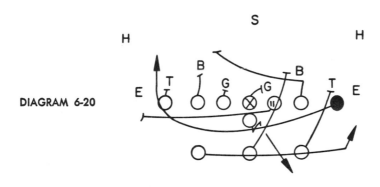

DIAGRAM 6-20

7

The Triple Option Series

What Is the Triple Option Series?

The Triple Option requires a reading or keying on certain defensive people. Two defensive men on the line of scrimmage are not blocked by the offensive team. The first defensive man past the nose of the defensive tackle is not touched and the next man out does not have to be blocked. (This will be mentioned later in the chapter.) The quarterback can either hand the football off to the offensive diving back according to the move of the first option man, or he can keep, or pitch on the movements of the next defensive opponent.

Strengths of the Triple Option Series

There are many strengths to the triple option attack. The following are some of the thoughts and ideas behind such an effective threat.

1. It is easy to learn and understand for the offensive line. Blocking rules are simple and not difficult to execute.
2. Since the offensive attack has numerous plays at its disposal, it is the only series that has to be utilized by the offense.
3. Only the defensive players inside of the offensive tackle have to be blocked along the line of scrimmage.
4. The other defensive players outside the offensive tackle do not have to be forced or driven off the line of scrimmage.
5. Offensive receivers release from the line of scrimmage forcing the defensive secondary to remain back or retreat. (It may cause the defense to revert to zone secondary coverage.)
6. Maximum speed is utilized along the entire line.
7. Offensive backs are thrusting straight ahead.
8. Quick and fast option plays develop along the line of scrimmage.
9. Faking and deception occur along the line and not in the backfield.
10. Usually the best back is utilized to run the football especially with the quick hitting play.

11. Average personnel can easily be employed with the entire series. Brute force and power, etc., is not necessary.
12. Counters, reverses, and other options can easily be used with the triple option play.
13. Play action passes can be used easily, because the offensive receivers are continually releasing from the line of scrimmage on every play.

Formations Necessary

The formations that can be employed are numerous. Many sets can be tight while others can be wide to one or both sides. It is necessary, however, there be at least two offensive backs behind the quarterback for the triple option to work. One back will be the dive man while the other is the pitch man. Usually when tight sets are employed, the offense will remain on the ground and have three offensive backs behind the quarterback in the backfield. With wide formations, however, the coach is going to throw the ball, spread the defense, so he can attack other specific weaknesses of a defense. Diagrams 7-1 through 7-6 are some of the numerous formations that can be used by the football coach.

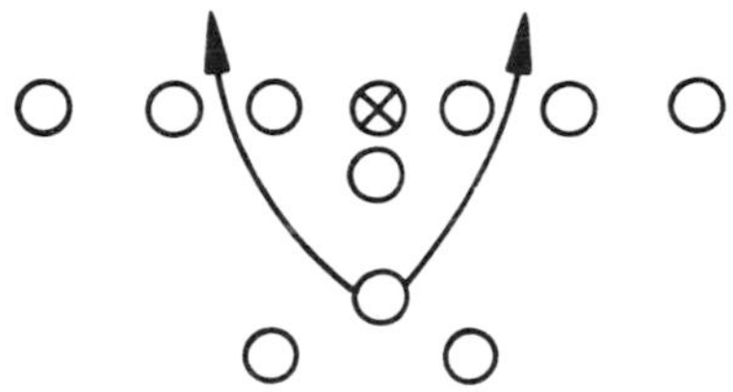

DIAGRAM 7-1
The Wishbone "T" Formation

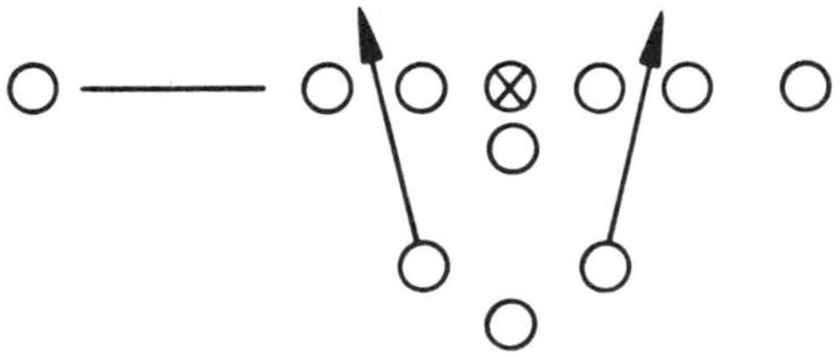

DIAGRAM 7-2
"T" Formation—Split End
(Fullback Deep)

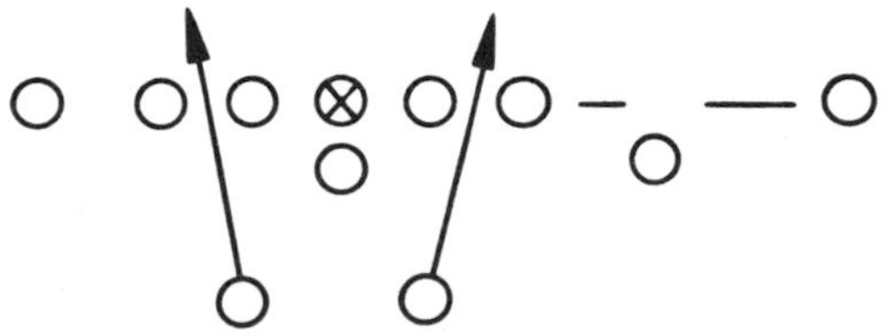

DIAGRAM 7-3
Slot Formation—Split Backfield

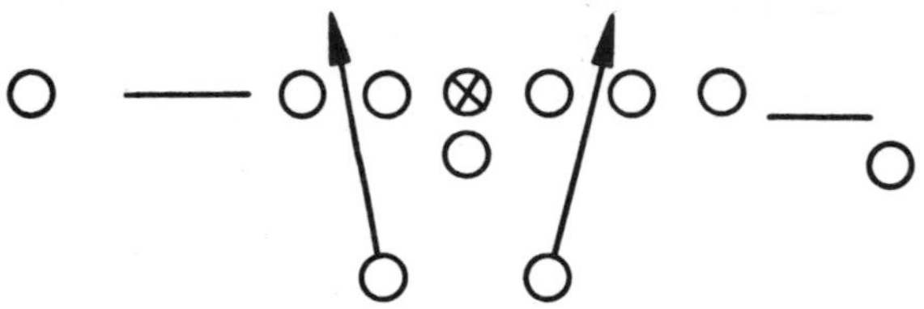

DIAGRAM 7-4
Pro Formation—Split Backfield

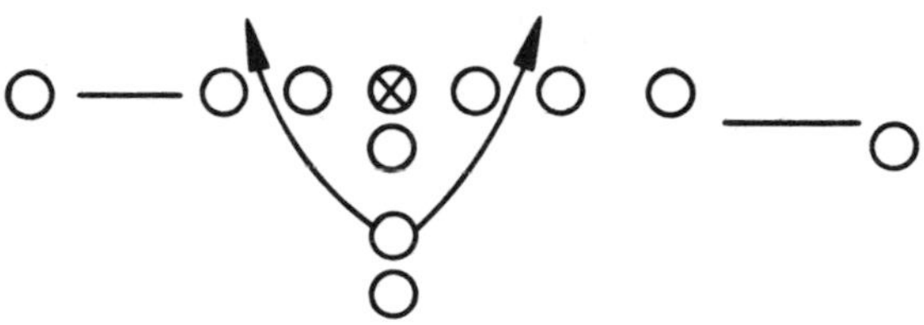

DIAGRAM 7-5
Pro "I" Formation

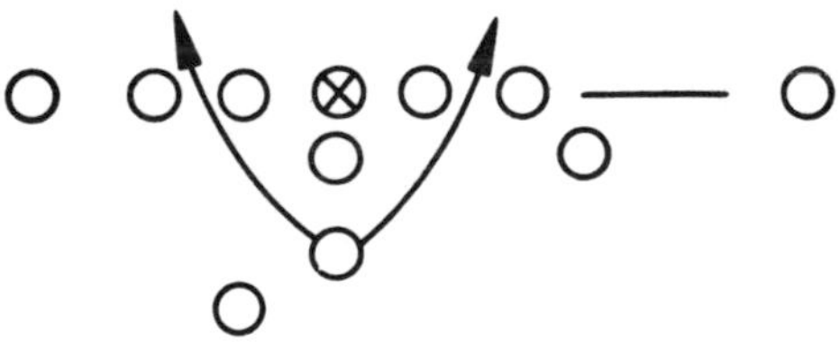

DIAGRAM 7-6
Wishbone Slot Formation

Importance of Offensive Splitting

Offensive splits are important. Usually the basic split between the linemen is three feet. However, this can vary according to the defensive set, team playing and offensive play executed. Diagram 7-7 illustrates the splits of the offensive line.

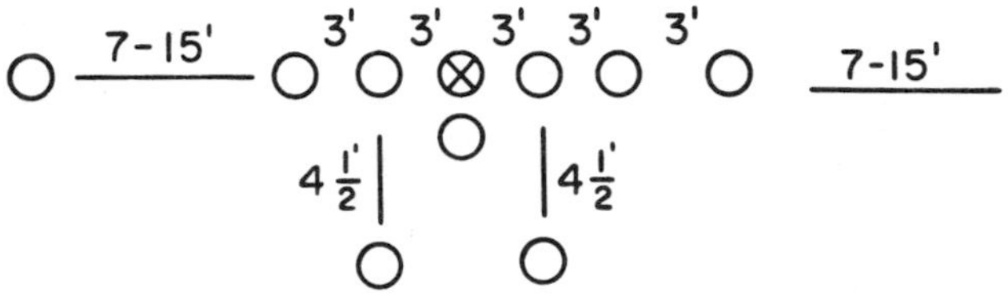

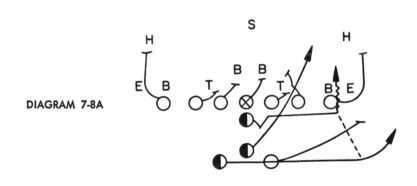

DIAGRAM 7-7

THE PLAY OF THE TRIPLE OPTION

The triple option play is illustrated in Diagram 7-8A and 7-8B, both from a tight and wide formation. The rules, execution, and coaching points of the triple option play follow. The wide set triple option will be explained. (Look to Diagrams 7-18 A, B, and C for blocking versus all defenses and adjustments.)

DIAGRAM 7-8A

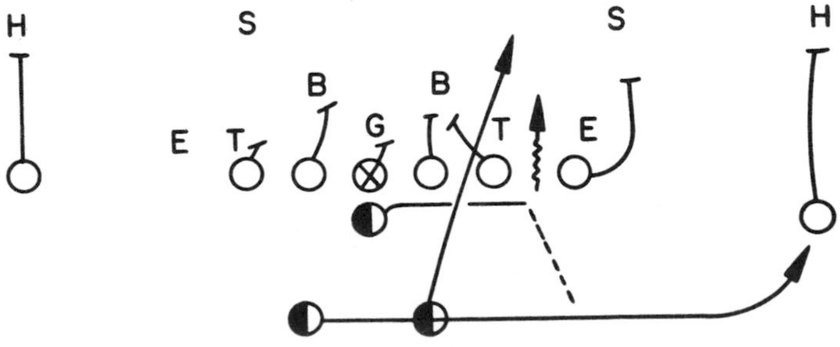

DIAGRAM 7-8B

OFFENSIVE LINE

Onside End

Rule: Release and block force man or ¼ area.

Execution: The tight end can split if necessary to cause the defensive personnel to adjust. Weaknesses may result. Release to the outside putting pressure on the defensive end. Do not let him come hard to the inside for the quarterback. Go around the defensive end low and come upfield in a good football position ready to chop the force man down. If he does not come, go for the defensive safety man. Some important points are: release hard with speed and be alert; keep a wide base; head up and stay low before throwing block.

Coaching Point: Do not lean in the offensive stance. If an eight-man front shows, the tight end can split partially.

Onside Tackle

Rule: Inside gap, linebacker.

Execution: On the snap of the ball, the tackle will block his rule. If man in gap, block him. Do not allow any pentration. First step is with the near foot. If defensive man attempts to penetrate, throw head in front and stop pressure. Once this is done, cut off pursuit by swinging body around. If no penetration is made by the defensive man, then slide the head to his back and drive man to inside. If linebacker, then screen man off to inside. Cut him down if necessary. Keep body under control and stay low.

Coaching Points: Keep head up when coming down on defender inside. Must screen this area off at all costs. These men cannot stop the triple option. Fire-out hard and low. Stay off the ground; use hands if necessary.

Onside Guard

Rule: Block number 1 man.

Execution: The offensive guard blocks his assignment according to where the defensive number 1 man aligns. If inside gap, do not allow penetration. If over, fire-out hard directly at man and tie his legs up. Do not allow pursuit by this man. Slide the head to the outside and stay with defender. Scramble block if bigger and stronger.

Coaching Points: Listen for call by offensive tackle for any other blocking combination. Stay low on block and do not go to the ground. If linebacker is number 1 man fire-out hard at man and do not allow pursuit of any type. Keep defender low and screen him off.

Center

Rule: Number 0 and onside gap.

Execution: Make a good snap with the quarterback. Fire-out for the defensive opponent. If over, reach for man and cut him off. Do not allow any penetration by this man. If no man over, reach for the onside gap and do not allow any penetration due to stunts, blitzes, etc.

Coaching Points: Aim the head into the midsection of the middle guard and slide to the outside. Do not go to the ground or lose contact. If going for onside gap, throw head in front and attempt to stop pursuit of the defender.

Offside Guard

Rule: Block number 1 man.

Execution: On the snap of the ball, block the number 1 man wherever he may be. If in onside gap, stop penetration at all costs. Throw head in front. If linebacker, attempt to screen him off. Take a cut off-point on the man. He cannot be driven past hole; he must be screened or fenced off.

Coaching Points: Fire-out hard and low for the defensive counterpart. Keep a wide base, shoulders square, tail down, and head up to make a good block. Read the defense for the proper block.

Offside Tackle

Rule: Block number 2 man.

Execution: On the snap of the ball, block the number 2 defensive man wherever he may be. Stop any type of pursuit course by this man. If the defensive man is in the onside gap, stop penetration by stepping with near foot and placing head in front of defensive man. Try to come up on man on other side to stop pursuit. If linebacker, screen man off.

Coaching Points: Fire-out hard and low at defensive man. Throw head for midsection and slide to the onside. Use hands if going to the ground. Keep a wide base and head up when performing the block.

Offside End

Rule: Block outside ⅓ or run streak pattern.

Execution: On the snap of the ball, release from the line of scrimmage and go hard for the defensive halfback. Make the defensive man retreat back. Once the play develops and the halfback makes a move, chop man down. Keep head in front. Do not go to ground by blocking low. Stay up in the air and throw high at the chest of halfback.

Coaching Points: If running a streak, go hard on pattern. Do not slow up. Defender will eventually know when the play is going away. If blocking, go full speed. It does not do any good to slow down. If the split end does a good job, the counters and counter-options execute well.

OFFENSIVE BACKFIELD

Flanker

Rule: Block outside ⅓.

Execution: On the snap of the ball, release from the line of scrimmage and go hard for the man who retreats into the deep outside ⅓ area. Make the defensive man retreat back. When the defensive halfback makes a move toward the ballcarrier, be in a good ready position to cut him down. Stay low, head up, with a wide base to cut in either direction. Do not miss this block.

Coaching Points: Release hard from the line of scrimmage as if the play were a pass route. Line up as wide as possible to force the defensive secondary to spread and make it difficult for the defenders covering inside to stay with the flanker out.

Fullback (Right Halfback)

Rule: Run for the guard-tackle gap.

Execution: The alignment of the offensive back is directly behind the offensive guard at a depth of approximately 4 to 4½ yards. The feet of the halfback are even with that of the offensive guard. On the snap of the ball, the back explodes from his stance and slashes between the guard and tackle seam. His elbow comes up and feels the ball into his stomach. A slight squeeze is added. He runs hard for the hole.

Coaching Points: Depth of the alignment may be determined by the speed of the back. Do not come up high after coming out of stance. Keep elbow high so fumbles will not occur. The back will know if he receives the ball if he feels the quarterback's hands leave the football. The back should slap his elbow with the bottom hand in order to get a good grip of the football also.

Quarterback

Rule: Key the first man outside the offensive tackle.

Execution: After receiving the snap from the center, the quarterback should drive off his opposite foot and at the same time eye the man he must read. The step is down the line. The quarterback will get to a position behind the outside foot of the offensive guard and point the football at the defensive tackle. He will then mesh with the diving halfback. If the defensive tackle does not come for the ball or halfback, the quarterback will give him the football. However, if the defensive opponent comes for the diving man, the quarterback will take the ball out and step around the collision point between the defensive man and the diving halfback. After the quarterback removes the football, he will go for the next defensive man (end) and option him.

As the quarterback reaches the next option man, he will read his movement. If the defensive man comes for the quarterback, he will pitch the football to the trailing halfback. However, if the defensive man floats, comes across the line, or retreats, etc., the quarterback will keep the football and run.

Coaching Points: The quarterback should deliver the football with a soft touch to the trailing halfback. The pitch should be made out in front of the man and not behind him. The ball should not go out hard. Stay in a good ready position when optioning. Do not come up high or be off balance.

Halfback

Execution: The offensive halfback aligns the same as the other halfback; directly behind the offensive guard approximately 4 to 4½ yards in depth. On the snap of the ball, the halfback pushes off his outside foot and runs the chalk line parallel with the quarterback. He should not come forward nor gain depth in the backfield. He should position himself in front and on the outside hip of the quarterback about 4 yards in depth from him. He should not get close, because the defensive end has the opportunity to break up the play.

Coaching Points: Do not lean in the stance to show direction of play. After getting pitch from quarterback, read the blocks of the tight end and flanker. Be a broken field runner and go for daylight. Attempt to stay outside after receiving pitch.

Variations of the Triple Option

On the offensive line there can occur a combination of different blocking schemes and calls. In many cases, there can be week-by-week adjustments on the line or these maneuvers can be called during a game. Diagrams 7-9 A, B, and C illustrate a combination block (combo) that can be utilized. The offensive guard blocks on the defensive down lineman in his area while the offensive tackle picks up the linebacker. As an example, versus the 4-4, the guard is blocking the number 2 man and similar blocks result with the 5-3 and 5-4 alignments, etc. (versus the 5-4 only if the defensive tackle shifts to the inside). This is accomplished when the offensive tackle splits out because of an odd nine man front. In the cases illustrated, the offensive tackle can easily "bump" the defensive tackle to the inside before blocking the defensive linebacker.

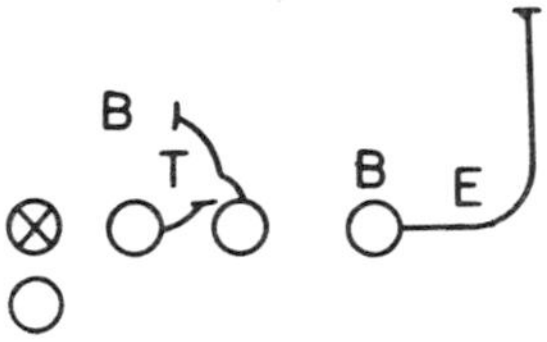

DIAGRAM 7-9A
4-4 Defense

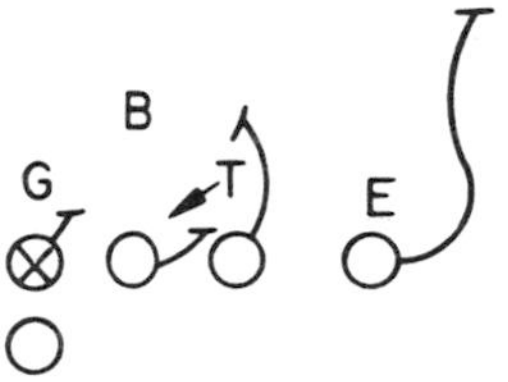

DIAGRAM 7-9B
5-3 Defense

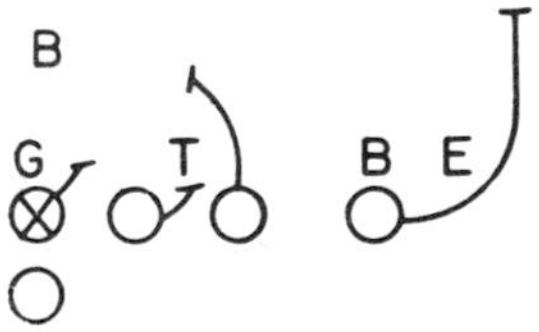

DIAGRAM 7-9C
5-4 Defense

Versus a 5-4-2 defense, the offensive tackle may not be able to release inside for the linebacker, because the defensive tackle will hold him up. However, at times the tackle can easily release to the outside as shown in Diagram 7-10A. If this is done and the defensive tackle holds him in the line of scrimmage, the offensive tackle should stay with this man and block him (Diagram 7-10B).

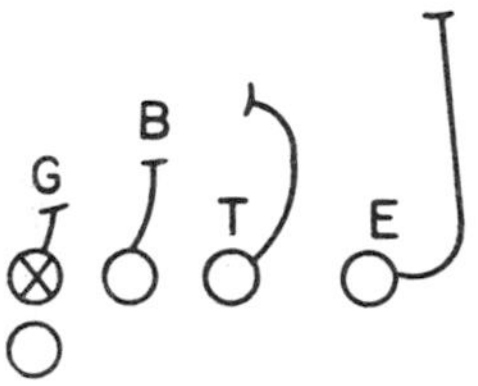

DIAGRAM 7-10A
5-4 Defense

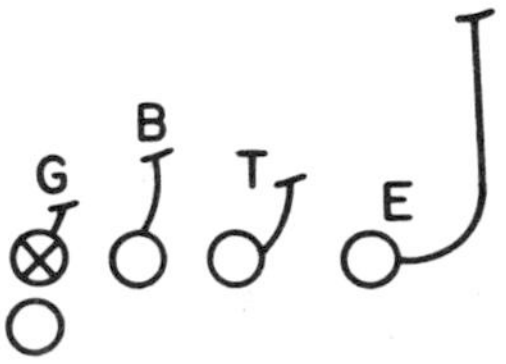

DIAGRAM 7-10B
5-4 Defense

Double-team blocking can easily be accomplished. This is usually done when a defensive tackle is positioned in the gap between the offensive guard and tackle. An offensive call can be made—Diagrams 7-11 A, B, and C illustrate the blocking.

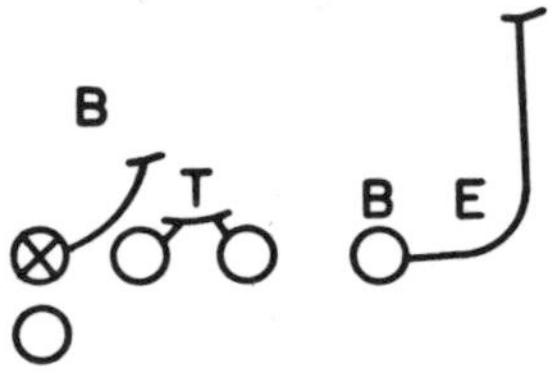

DIAGRAM 7-11A
4-4 Defense

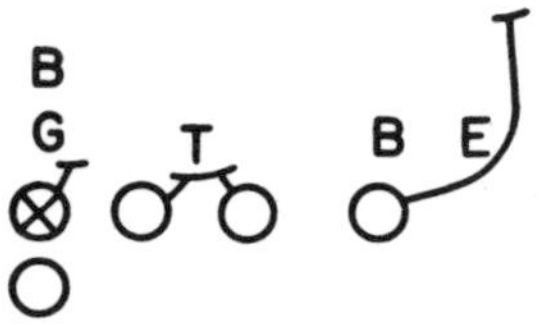

DIAGRAM 7-11B
5-3 Defense

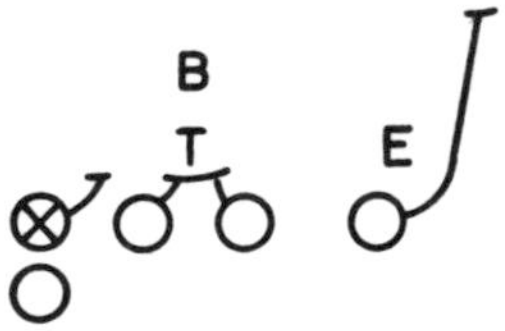

DIAGRAM 7-11C
5-4 Stack Look

Defensive stunts, blitzes, and adjustments can cause havoc if not properly prepared. The offensive line should be thoroughly ready for such defensive movements. An "area" call can be installed if this should occur. Diagrams 7-12 A and B illustrate two defensive maneuvers with the offensive line blocking the stunts.

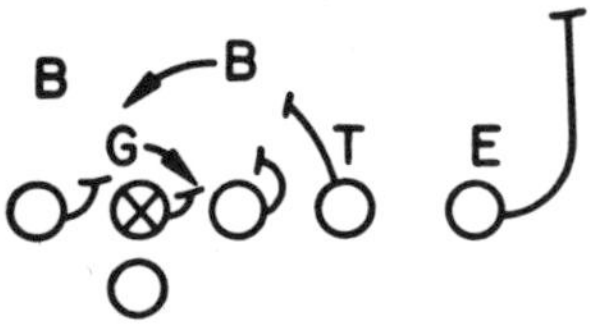

DIAGRAM 7-12A
5-4 Stunt

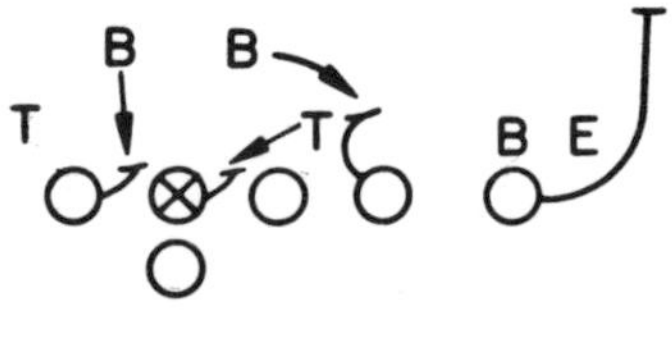

DIAGRAM 7-12B
4-4 Stunt

While the offensive guard blocks the number 1 defensive man, there are instances where he can help block with the offensive center (Diagrams 7-13 A and B). Word calls can be employed for the block if necessary.

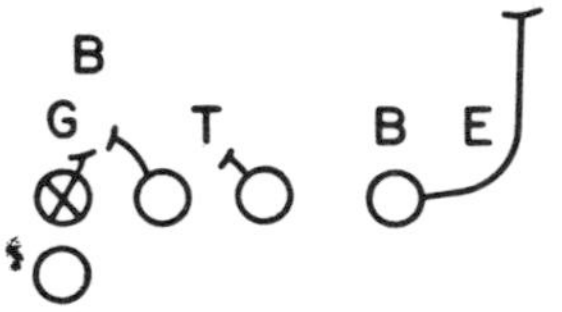

DIAGRAM 7-13A
5-3 Defense

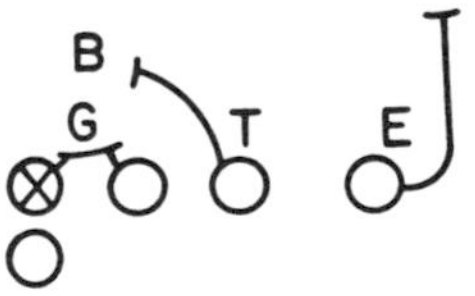

DIAGRAM 7-13B
5-4 Stack Defense

The offside tackle, instead of blocking the defensive number 2 man, can release downfield and block the middle ⅓ of the defensive secondary (Diagram 7-14). Another offensive variation is to switch the assignments of the offensive tight end and flanker back. The flanker can block the force man while the tight end blocks the deep outside ⅓ area (Diagram 7-15). If the inside linebackers cannot be blocked, the offensive tight end can release as usual, but come inside to stop pursuit (Diagram 7-16).

DIAGRAM 7-14

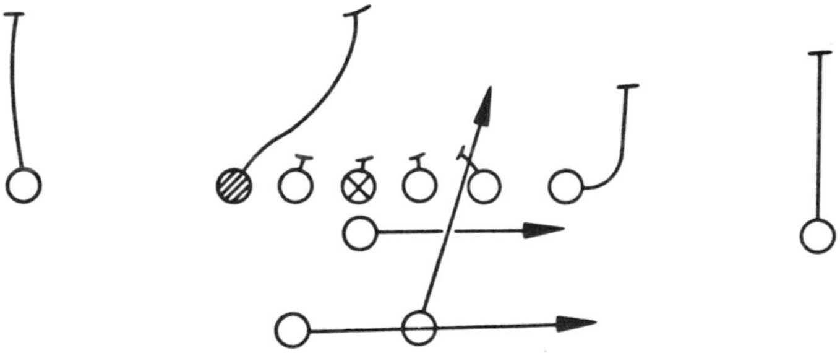

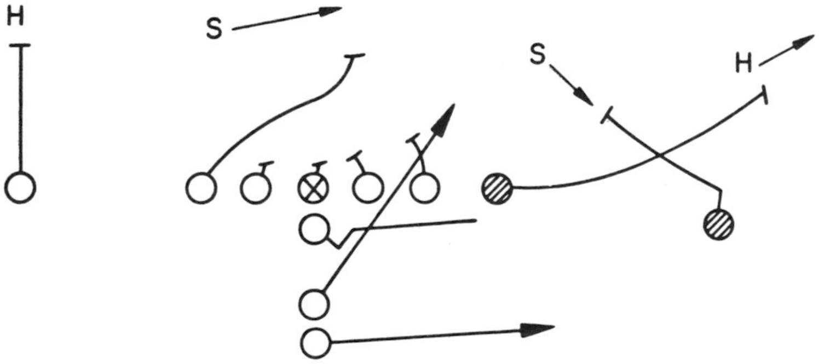

DIAGRAM 7-15

DIAGRAM 7-16

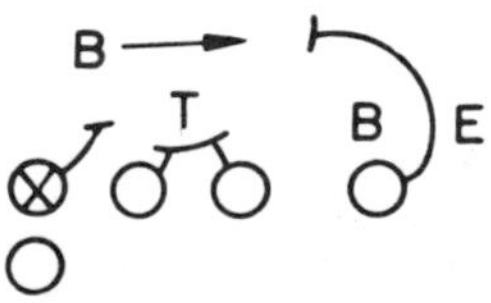

If the ride is to be accomplished with a fullback and quarterback, the mesh and ride can vary. Instead of the quarterback joining the dive man on the line of scrimmage, the quarterback could open-step back and meet the fullback deeper in the backfield. If this occurs, a longer ride will exist between these two men. Diagram 7-17 illustrates this offensive mesh technique. While there are numerous coaches who have the *quarterback* decide who receives the ball, there are a few coaches who have the diving *back* read the movements of the defensive line and take the ball on this cue. This is drilled repeatedly by the coach also. A different technique is to tell the quarterback to definitely pitch the ball on the second option, *unless* the defensive man goes directly for the pitch man. This small coaching point makes the quarterback conscious of pitching on every option. It is best for the quarterback to make a quicker choice, rather than *not* knowing what to do and causing confusion.

DIAGRAM 7-17

Diagrams 7-18 A, B, and C indicate the offensive blocking and quarterback reads versus three defenses.

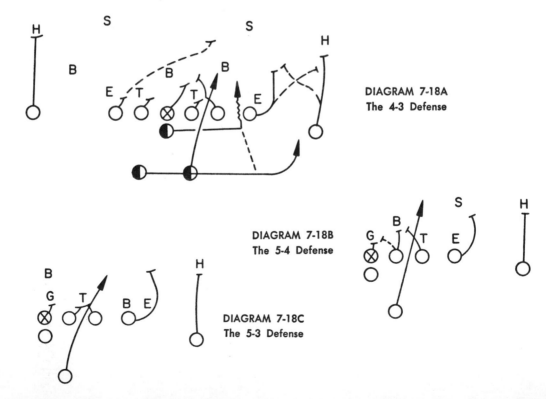

DIAGRAM 7-18A
The 4-3 Defense

DIAGRAM 7-18B
The 5-4 Defense

DIAGRAM 7-18C
The 5-3 Defense

The Triple Option to the Split End Side

Diagrams 7-19 A and B illustrate the triple option executed to the side of the split end. All the rules remain similar to those to the tight end position. In this option, the tight end is not employed. The quarterback steps out and keys the first man outside the offensive tackle. The three-way option then proceeds as previously mentioned.

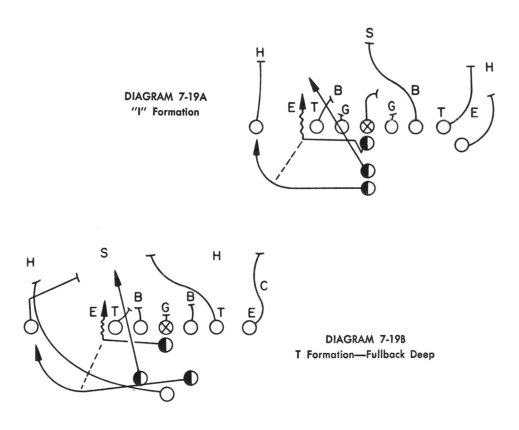

DIAGRAM 7-19A
"I" Formation

DIAGRAM 7-19B
T Formation—Fullback Deep

Halfback Counter

An excellent counter play is shown in Diagrams 7-20 A and B. The quarterback open-steps as if beginning the triple option. He initiates one step with the next foot, reverse pivots, and hands back to the tailback. The ballcarrier takes a jab step in the direction of the flow, then cuts straight up the middle, keeping the shoulders parallel to the line of scrimmage. His aiming point is the center's near foot. He will cut off the block of the offensive center and guard to that side. The blocking on the line of scrimmage is one-on-one. However, step-around maneuvers can be utilized when certain defenses are employed.

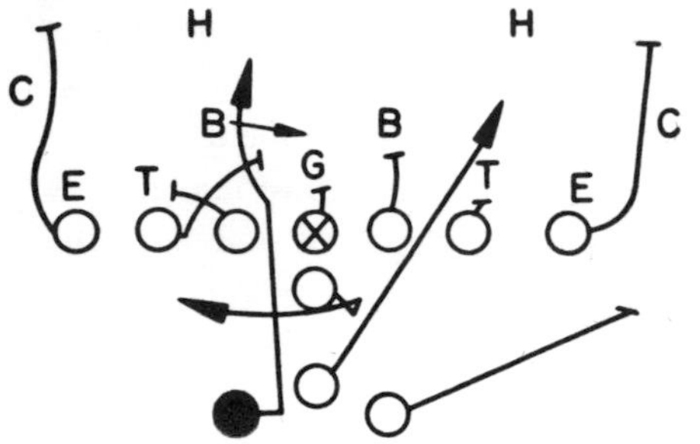

DIAGRAM 7-20A

DIAGRAM 7-20B

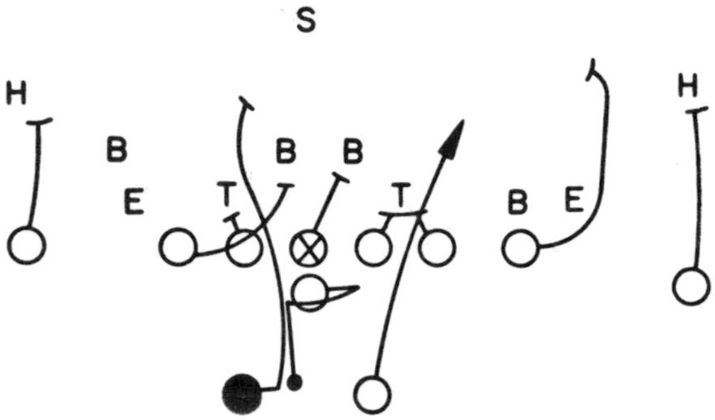

The Counter Option

The counter option materializes from the counter halfback play. The quarterback initiates two short jab steps, fakes the dive, pivots off the second step, and fakes the counter halfback dive. He continues down the line at the defensive end. This is a single option with no three-way option involved. Diagram 7-21 illustrates the counter option to the split end side while Diagram 7-22 indicates the same play to the tight end position.

In Diagram 7-21 a split backfield is shown and there is no actual dive man, because he must be the trailing halfback for the pitch. However, with three offensive backfield men (Diagram 7-22) the dive and counter play can be faked. Diagram 7-23 indicates the same play as shown in Diagram 7-22 except that the fullback does not go forward, but jab steps in the direction of the flow. He

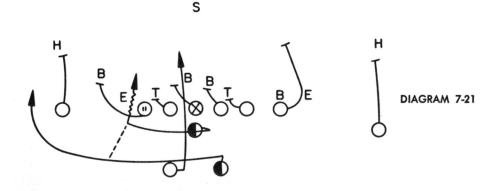

DIAGRAM 7-21

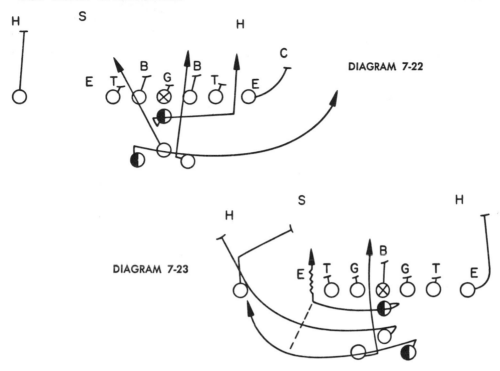

DIAGRAM 7-22

DIAGRAM 7-23

pivots on this foot and blocks the defensive halfback. This, therefore, becomes an added blocker in front of the ballcarrier. The offensive linemen block straight ahead and attempt to stay with their defensive counterparts as long as possible due to the timing in the backfield.

The Straight Dive and Single Option

A very simple play that definitely results in the dive, although it looks as if it were the triple option, is the straight-ahead dive. One-on-one blocking is utilized versus all defenses. From the triple option can be executed the single option on the defensive end also. Only one option is utilized. The offensive players know a triple option will not occur. Diagram 7-24A illustrates the dive while Diagram 7-24B shows the straight option.

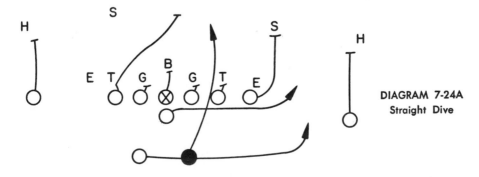

DIAGRAM 7-24A
Straight Dive

DIAGRAM 7-24B
Straight Option

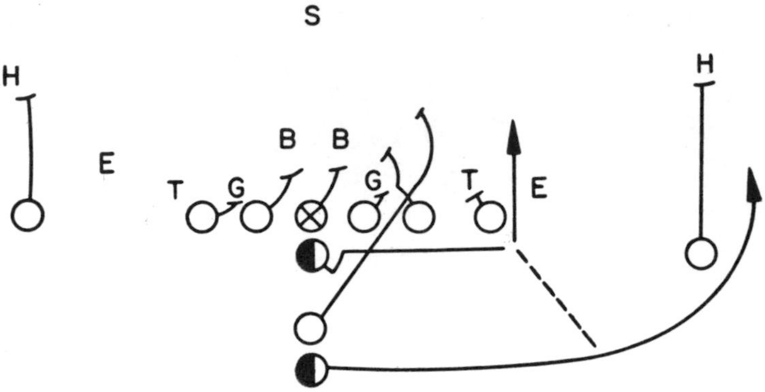

The Quickie Pass

Another excellent play from the triple option sequence of plays is the quickie pass to the tight or split end. This pass can be executed two ways. The play can be a definite pass or the quarterback can read the reactions of the defensive team and either hand the ball off to the dive man, option on the defensive end, or pass the ball to one of the receivers. Of course the easiest method is to have a definite pass play (Diagram 7-25). The split end quickie pass is illustrated in Diagram 7-26.

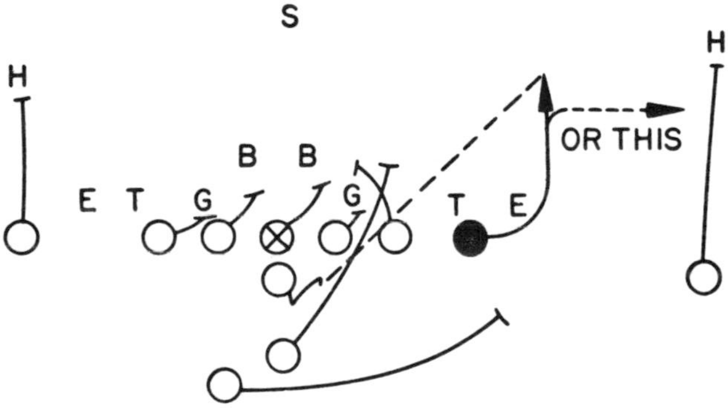

DIAGRAM 7-25

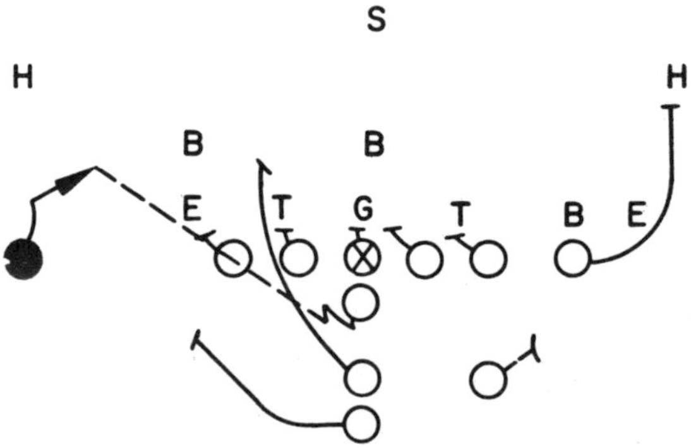

DIAGRAM 7-26

There are a few coaches who employ the quickie pass with the triple option theory. Diagram 7-27A illustrates the triple option look. The quarterback is reading the movements of the outside linebacker. If the linebacker comes hard for the dive man, the quarterback will throw the ball to the tight end. However, if the linebacker drops back with the tight end, the quarterback will hand the ball off to the diving halfback (Diagram 7-27B).

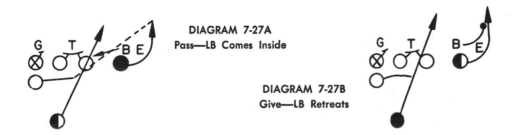

DIAGRAM 7-27A
Pass—LB Comes Inside

DIAGRAM 7-27B
Give—LB Retreats

The throw-back quickie pass can be accomplished also. Diagram 7-28A illustrates the throw-back pass to the split end, while Diagram 7-28B shows the throw-back pass to the tight end. Both are excellent when the defense is pursuing quickly to the direction of the flow.

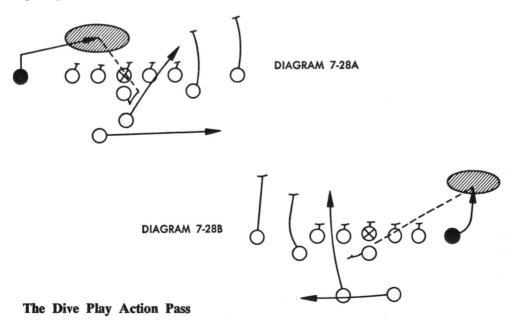

DIAGRAM 7-28A

DIAGRAM 7-28B

The Dive Play Action Pass

An excellent play action pass is when the quarterback comes down the line and fakes the veer or dive play and drops back to pass the ball. Any number of pass routes and patterns can be employed. Diagram 7-29A illustrates the flanker running on a pass route while the tight end swings to the outside and streaks downfield. The quarterback looks to the post route first and the streak second. The dive man can sneak out into the flat or execute a hook pattern also. (Diagram 7-29B shows another pattern.)

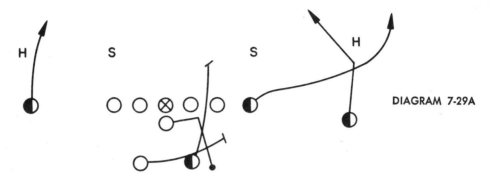

DIAGRAM 7-29A

DIAGRAM 7-29B

Counter Option Pass

The counter option pass is utilized from the counter option run explained previously. The play can be executed to either side of the offensive center. It is an excellent play action pass which must be drilled repeatedly. The ball will either be thrown to the receiver or optioned at the defensive end. In Diagram 7-30, the quarterback executes his counter maneuver. After he initiates a good fake with the halfback diving into the line, he reads the tight end. If he is not covered, the quarterback will throw the ball to him. However, if he is covered, the quarterback will continue down the line of scrimmage and perform an option at the defensive end. If the tight end is covered, he will break outside. The quarterback may pass the ball to him at this position also.

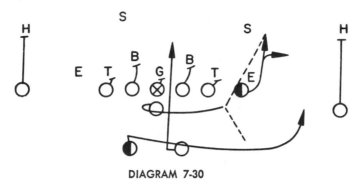

DIAGRAM 7-30

The Counter Halfback Pass

The counter halfback pass is shown in Diagram 7-31. The quarterback initiates his fake and drops back to look for any open receiver. He should read the split end first and the trailing tight end second.

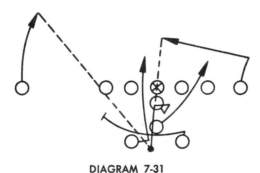

DIAGRAM 7-31

The Outside Triple Option

The outside triple option play is very similar to the triple option. The reason for such a play is obvious. In the previous triple options, the first option man (for example the defensive tackle in the 5-4 defense) was being exploited by the offense. During a course of a ball game, this defensive man will begin to come hard to the inside in an effort to stop the dive back. If the offense is having a difficult time with this maneuver, the outside triple option should execute well.

In this case, the offensive tight end will not release, but will help block on the line of scrimmage. The dive back will have an aiming point of one gap out (the tackle-end seam). The triple option has now moved one hole outside, while the quarterback performs the same duties mentioned previously. Diagram 7-32 indicates the quarterback's read on the defensive end. If the end comes hard for the dive back, the quarterback will keep the ball and sprint outside for the next contain man. He will option this defensive man with the trailing halfback.

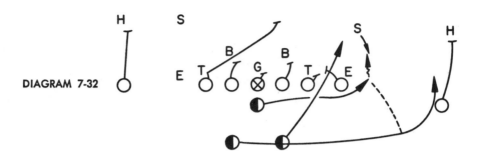

DIAGRAM 7-32

The Inside and Outside Veer (Dive)

The outside dive coordinates with the outside triple option, except the dive back definitely receives the ball from the quarterback and the offensive line blocks one-on-one with their defensive counterparts. The inside veer calls for the diving halfback to cut inside. This is usually called when the defensive front men are over-pursuing and the back cuts inside where the defensive men have left. Straight blocks should be used; however, step-around and trap maneuvers can be employed. Diagram 7-33 illustrates the outside dive while Diagrams 7-34 A and B show the inside veer cut.

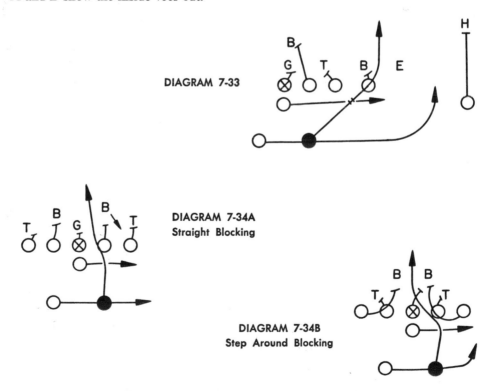

DIAGRAM 7-33

DIAGRAM 7-34A
Straight Blocking

DIAGRAM 7-34B
Step Around Blocking

The Flip Reverse

An excellent reverse from the triple option look is illustrated in Diagram 7-35. The quarterback steps out and meshes with the fullback. He takes the ball after the ride and continues at the defensive end as if he is going to option him. The split end, during this time, comes back toward the formation. As he enters the quarterback's area, he receives a pitch from him. The split end attempts to get outside. The offensive tackle peels back on the defensive end while the offensive guard and center go hard to the outside. This can be executed from a flanker formation also.

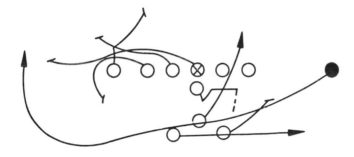

DIAGRAM 7-35

The Quick Pitch Series

One of the better offensive series in football is the Quick Pitch sequence of plays. Surprisingly, however, there has been little written or said about the Quick Pitch. It has been overlooked in articles, books, and speeches and this is probably due to its simplicity of play. The Quick Pitch series can be a very potent offensive attack. It can break open a game with its quickness and surprise and give the offense an opportunity to score with speed and deceptiveness.

Strengths and When to Attack with the Quick Pitch Series

The strengths and when to attack with the Quick Pitch sequence of plays are as follows.

1. It gets outside with speed and quickness.
2. Defensive personnel must move quick on pursuit to get to the ballcarrier.
3. It is excellent as an element of surprise.
4. It is good when the defensive secondary is playing off or back considerably from the line of scrimmage usually when anticipating a pass.
5. When defensive ends are crashing and it is difficult to run inside, that is the time to call the Quick Pitch.
6. It is good when the defensive ends are waiting, but not floating or going wide.
7. When the defense is playing tight for the inside running game the Quick Pitch is excellent.
8. It is good when the defense is stunting, angling, stacking, jumping, etc., and the offensive linemen can not block straight ahead.
9. Split ends, put out flankers, twins, slots, etc., to best capitalize on the adjustments of the defense.

Formations for the Quick Pitch Series

While there are numerous formations that can be utilized an important point necessary for the Quick Pitch to be successful is the tailback must be at least four yards off the line of scrimmage. The tailback's stance should be straddling the inside leg of the offensive tackle. This may vary with offensive line splits and coaching techniques, etc.

The Quick Pitch can be successful with an offensive end split wide or tight also. In many cases, this will be determined on how the defense adjusts and aligns to the offensive formation. For an example, in Diagram 8-1 and 8-2 a slot formation is illustrated. Complete rotation is shown in Diagram 8-1 and a four-deep is employed in Diagram 8-2. The coach, therefore, may quick pitch to the weak side versus a fully rotated secondary, but can toss to the slot versus a four-deep look. Any other formation can easily be used.

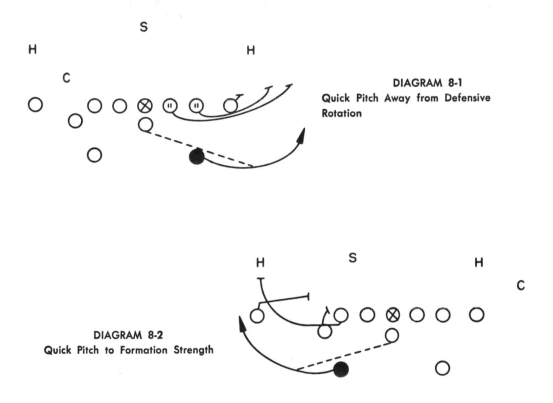

DIAGRAM 8-1
Quick Pitch Away from Defensive Rotation

DIAGRAM 8-2
Quick Pitch to Formation Strength

THE PLAY OF THE QUICK PITCH

While there are numerous variations of the Quick Pitch play, the following (Diagrams 8-3A and B) is one method. Other possible ways are explained later in the chapter. The offensive rules with techniques and coaching points are included.

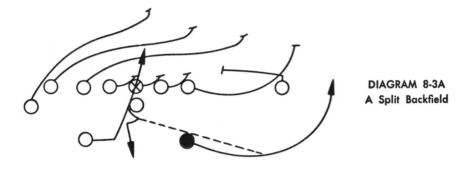

DIAGRAM 8-3A
A Split Backfield

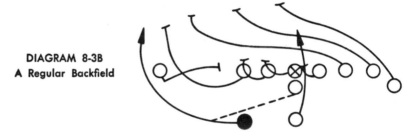

DIAGRAM 8-3B
A Regular Backfield

OFFENSIVE LINE

Onside Split End

Rule: Block first man down inside on the line of scrimmage. If no end man, seal inside pursuit (or walk away man). If double covered, release and block outside ⅓.

Execution: From a good two- or three-point stance, the split end should come down hard inside and cut down the defensive end. He must throw a cross-body block and put the head in front.

Coaching Points: Cut the split down. Be able to see front numbers before throwing block. DO NOT CLIP.

Onside Tackle

Rule: Pull and block the first man outside the split end's block.

Execution: From a good three-point stance, the tackle should pull the outside arm, snap the head, and initiate a deep pull-lead step in the direction of the pitch. Get depth and pull around the split end's block. Block the defensive halfback unless defensive pursuit deems otherwise.

Coaching Points: Get quick and fast pull. If the defensive end comes across hard and the split end cannot block him, chop him down. If split end is double covered, block first man out (Diagram 8-4).

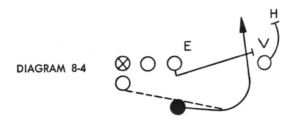

DIAGRAM 8-4

Onside Guard

Rule: Pull, reach, release.

Execution: The guard should pull from his position and reach for the man over or in the gap nearest the next onside offensive linemen. If no man shows, release downfield and chop first man that comes into the area.

Coaching Points: Pull as did the offensive tackle, but reach for the next man over. Attempt to turn opponent inside and cut off pursuit. Stay on feet and under control. Do not go to the ground.

Center

Rule: Same as onside guard.

Execution: Same as onside guard.

Coaching Points: Same as onside guard.

Offside Guard

Rule: Same as onside guard.

Execution: Same as onside guard.

Coaching Points: Same as onside guard.

Offside Tackle

Rule: Crossfield and chop.

Execution: The offside tackle should take an inside release, stay shallow to the line of scrimmage and chop down the first man that shows.

Coaching Points: Release hard and fast. Do not look at the ballcarrier, but sprint across-field, then turn up looking for different color jersey. Throw cross-body block high and hard and come down through man.

Offside End

Rule: Same as offside tackle.

Execution: Same as offside tackle.

Coaching Points: Same as offside tackle.

OFFENSIVE BACKFIELD

Wingback or Flanker

Rule: Same as offside tackle.

Execution: Same as offside tackle.

Coaching Points: Same as offside tackle.

Tailback

Execution: Ballcarrier—From a good offensive stance, the tailback should push off the inside foot with the first step being deep. He should belly for depth, keeping the palms up. Once he takes the pitch he should be a broken field runner. He must key the tackle's block and react accordingly.

Coaching Points: Must get depth on initial movement. Look the ball into the hands and tuck away. Try to get outside.

Fullback

Execution: On the snap of the ball (from a regular fullback position) the fullback should drive directly to the opposite side of the pitch, aiming for the leg of the offensive center. Make a good fake as if the ball is handed off.

Coaching Points: Go hard for the center area. Keep the head up, knees pumping, and make a good fake.

Quarterback

Execution: The quarterback reverse pivots after the snap and pitches the ball out and up. He flips the football and does not attempt to spin it. He should not execute any fake with the diving fullback. If the fullback is in a halfback position, the quarterback can then come back and fake the fullback trap. After this has been accomplished, he can drop back and fake the play action pass.

Coaching Points: Reverse pivot at a ¾ turn to get ball tossed. The hands and arms are utilized in an under pitched motion. After the pitch is executed the palms should be facing upward.

Diagrams 8-5 A, B, C, and D vividly illustrate the Quick Pitch blocking maneuvers versus the most often viewed defenses.

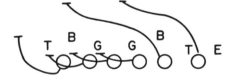

DIAGRAM 8-5A
Wide Tackle-6

DIAGRAM 8-5B
Split-6

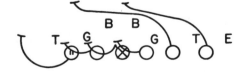

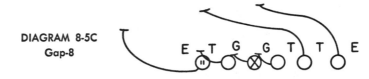

DIAGRAM 8-5C
Gap-8

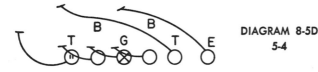

DIAGRAM 8-5D
5-4

Similarities in Other Quick Pitches

IN THE BACKFIELD

Different backfield maneuvers can be easily accomplished from the Quick Pitch play. Diagram 8-3A indicated a split backfield with the quarterback quick pitching the ball and coming back to fake the fullback trap. Diagram 8-6 shows another method in which the quarterback initiates the quick pitch, but fakes to the fullback off-tackle. Both these maneuvers will be explained later in the chapter.

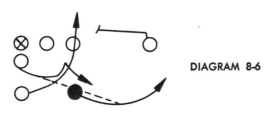

DIAGRAM 8-6

Another basic technique many coaches employ is the open-step maneuver for the quarterback. In this instance, the quarterback takes the snap from center and opens up his first step with the foot nearest the quick pitch ballcarrier. The quarterback underhands and flips the ball directly out similar to the reverse pivot (Diagram 8-7). The companion play from the open-step maneuver is some type of fake to the fullback over the onside offensive guard position.

ON THE LINE

There are a few coaches who pull the onside guard instead of the tackle as was previously illustrated. Diagram 8-8 indicates the pulling guard technique.

There are many coaches who employ both the onside guard and tackle in the Quick Pitch play which is shown in Diagram 8-9 also.

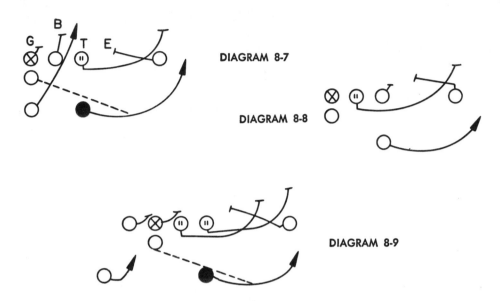

DIAGRAM 8-7

DIAGRAM 8-8

DIAGRAM 8-9

The split end has been indicated sealing inside. However, his rule can be to release from the line as if in a pass pattern and block the outside ⅓ area. With this maneuver, the onside tackle, guard, or both can seal the inside defensive pursuit.

The Quick Pitch can be accomplished toward the tight end or flanker side also. The tight end blocks the end man on the line of scrimmage with the guard, tackle or both pulling outside. Diagram 8-10 illustrates the quick pitch toward the tight end side with the flanker blocking the defensive halfback. The following are the rules versus all defenses.

Onside End: Block outside, over, wall inside.
Onside Tackle: Pull and kick out first man past end's block.
Onside Guard: Pull and seal inside.
Center: On gap, release.
Offside Guard: On gap, release.
Offside Tackle: Crossfield and chop.
Offside End: Slam, crossfield and chop.

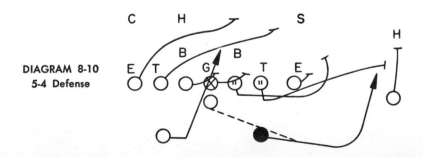

DIAGRAM 8-10
5-4 Defense

Once the defense utilizes maneuvers to halt the Quick Pitch, the other plays in the series must be employed. The plays used will be determined on the weaknesses developed in the defense caused in stopping the Quick Pitch. Attacking the defense properly is most important and knowing when and where to use intelligent strategy with the Quick Pitch sequence of plays is necessary in gaining good yardage.

Quick Pitch Pass

Many coaches utilize the open-step technique with the Quick Pitch, and after faking the toss, drops back by back-pedalling and hits the tight end coming across. The play is usually employed when the offense finds the linebackers are flowing quickly toward the pitch action. The offense, therefore, attacks the areas vacated by the linebackers (see Diagram 8-11).

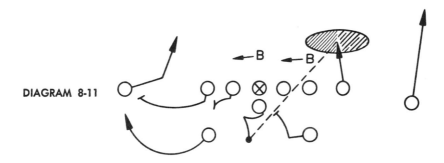

DIAGRAM 8-11

Middle Trap

The companion play most utilized, one continually faked from the Quick Pitch, is the middle fullback trap. The trap is used to attack the middle, because of the defensive linebacker and tackle pursuit to the Quick Pitch. Diagram 8-12 indicates the trap versus an "even" defense and Diagram 8-13 versus an "odd" look.

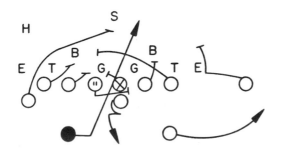

DIAGRAM 8-12
Split Backfield—Even Defense

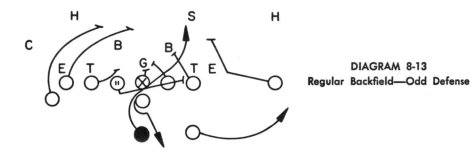

DIAGRAM 8-13
Regular Backfield—Odd Defense

If the fullback aligns in a split backfield set, he can use either an open-step and go directly to the area, or he can employ a cross-over, then another step, before he drives for the hole. In both instances, the ballcarrier must key the trap block by the offensive guard. From a regular backfield (Diagram 8-13) the fullback goes directly toward the center area and keys the trapper. If the defense is "even," the ball will likely go up the middle and if "odd," the ball-carrier will break wider.

Other blocking schemes for the same play are illustrated in Diagrams 8-14 and 8-15. If the trap does not work, the "double boom" block is an excellent change-up.

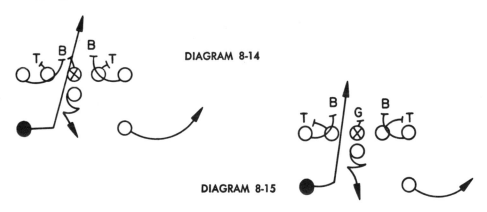

DIAGRAM 8-14

DIAGRAM 8-15

Slant Off-Tackle

The defensive end is the important factor in the Quick Pitch play. If the tailback, after receiving the toss, can get outside of him, the play has an excellent opportunity to gain yardage. However, if the defensive end floats or goes out hard to stop the Quick Pitch, the offense should attack inside the end (Diagram 8-16). Diagram 8-17 shows a quick slant play off-tackle. In many cases, the defensive end does not have to be blocked, because of the tailback's fake. The fullback, instead of faking up the middle, takes a cross-over lead step and bellys for daylight. The quarterback reverse pivots, fakes the quick pitch and hands off to the fullback. (Diagram 8-18A and B illustrate blocking versus other defenses.)

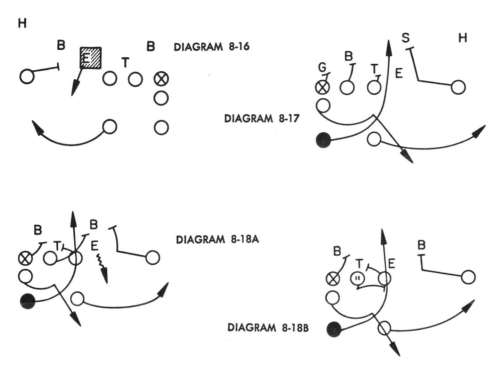

DIAGRAM 8-16

DIAGRAM 8-17

DIAGRAM 8-18A

DIAGRAM 8-18B

Slant Pass

Diagram 8-19 illustrates a simple pass from the slant off-tackle play. The tackle pulls as in the Quick Pitch, but blocks the defensive end. The fullback blocks the first man over the offensive tackle's area. The quarterback can call for any split end pattern and the tailback flares in the flat area.

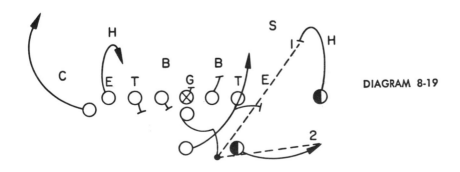

DIAGRAM 8-19

The Inside Slant Keep

The inside slant keep is similar to the slant off-tackle run for the offensive line. However, in the backfield, the quarterback fakes the Quick Pitch and keeps the ball. Again, the quarterback is attempting to attack inside the defensive end, because of his faking maneuvers outside. The fullback runs his normal drive fake up the middle area (Diagram 8-20).

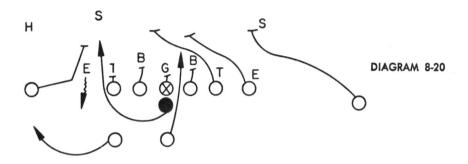

DIAGRAM 8-20

The Outside Slant Keep

The outside slant keep is an excellent play once the Quick Pitch series is gaining yardage and finding success. It is a highly skilled play, because it must be executed to perfection. It probably will not gain the yardage desired until after the Quick Pitch and the slant off-tackle play have been run a number of times. Diagram 8-21 illustrates the outside slant keep. The quarterback fakes the Quick Pitch, quickly rides the slant play (must be a good fake) and pushes off his inside foot. He puts the ball away in a bootleg fashion and sprints outside. The split end comes down as if blocking the quick pitch, but "seals inside pursuit." The most important man for this play is the tailback. The tailback fakes the toss, but holds and watches the defensive end. If the defensive end does not go for the slant fake of the halfback, he blocks him. However, if the defensive end goes for the slanting back, the tailback will continue on as an escort for the quarterback. The offensive linemen reach and the tackle pulls as in the Quick Pitch.

DIAGRAM 8-21

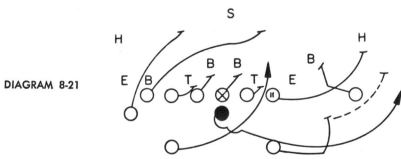

Slant Screen to Tight End

An excellent screen utilized with the Quick Pitch sequence of plays is the tight end screen off the quick pitch-slant pass fake. The quarterback fakes the toss, the slant off-tackle, and the slant pass. Once pressure is put on him, he will drop back and pass to the tight end (Diagram 8-22). The screen is employed in attacking the defense when much pressure and pursuit is being put on the Quick Pitch and its series of runs and passes.

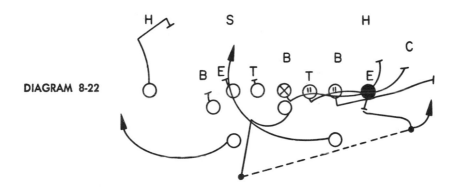

DIAGRAM 8-22

The Quick Pitch Delay

Diagram 8-23 illustrates the quick pitch delay. The quarterback fakes the quick pitch and the fullback trap. Once the fake has been executed, he pushes off his inside foot and starts back to pass. As he retreats, he quickly passes the ball out to the tailback who has delayed for a count after faking the toss. The most important block is the tight end's assignment. The tight end's rule is outside, over and he can either hook the end man or circle around as shown and chop him down. However, he must be quick and fast to circle his defensive opponent.

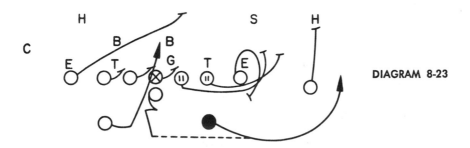

DIAGRAM 8-23

The Counter Pitch

Diagram 8-24 illustrates the counter pitch with the wing-back receiving the football. The quarterback fakes the Quick Pitch, fakes the trap and pitches to the wing as shown. The tailback cleans up on the defensive end first, then looks to the outside.

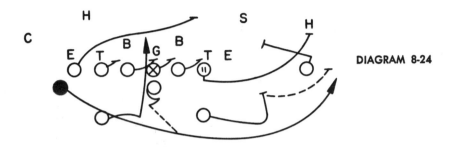

DIAGRAM 8-24

The Quick Pitch Option

The quick pitch option is similar to the swing option except the quarterback fakes the quick pitch and comes straight down the line for the defensive end (Diagram 8-25). If three offensive backs are employed in the backfield, the quarterback can fake to one of them up the middle area to hold the defensive linebackers.

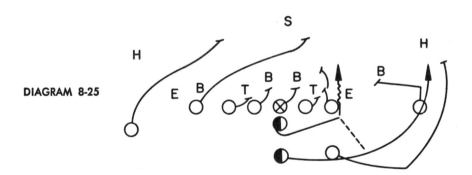

DIAGRAM 8-25

The Bang Off-Tackle and Pass

Diagram 8-26 illustrates the run of an off-tackle play with the halfback kicking the defensive end out. The quarterback, however, fakes the Quick Pitch as in the slant play and hopes to force the defensive end out making an easier block for the halfback. Diagram 8-27 indicates the play action pass from it.

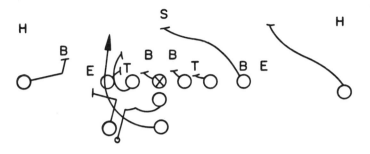

DIAGRAM 8-26

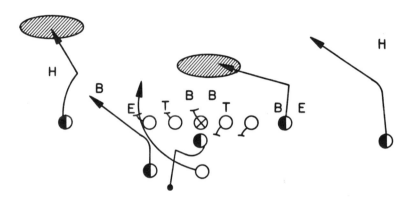

DIAGRAM 8-27

The Cross-Buck Series

In one form or another the Cross-Buck sequence of plays is employed by entirely every team in the country. It is utilized at the high school, college and professional level of football. All forms of backfield actions and line blocking patterns can be installed with the Cross-Buck series. The coach's Cross-Buck action will be determined by the type of formations and the personnel he has available. Numerous coaches will use only one play, while others will concentrate on a sequence of plays. Regular, split, "I," strong, etc., backfields can be used. A two- or a three-man backfield formation can be determined also. With three backs aligned together, a great deal of faking can be accomplished. If a certain ballplayer is a better runner than another, then a cross action may differ to get the ball to him.

What Is the Cross-Buck Series?

The Cross-Buck sequence is employed with either two or three offensive backs. In the action, one offensive back steps in front of another while going toward the line of scrimmage. He will either receive the football or fake into the line. The second offensive back will step behind the route of the first back (who is running in the opposite direction) and either receive the ball or fake into the line. If a third offensive back is utilized, he will usually run opposite the running lane of the second back. He may or may not receive the football (Diagram 9-1).

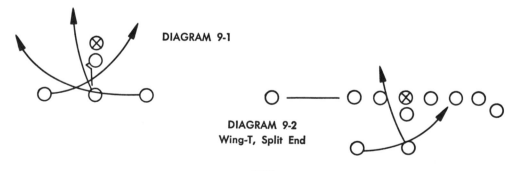

DIAGRAM 9-1

DIAGRAM 9-2
Wing-T, Split End

Strengths of the Cross-Buck Series

As with every offensive sequence of plays there are many strengths and weaknesses. Following are some of the strengths of the Cross-Buck series.

1. A good deal of faking and deception occur in the offensive backfield due to the crossing action utilized.
2. While faking is occurring, many blocking patterns and techniques can be used with the offensive line and backfield. This includes straight-ahead, cross, trap, double-team and power blocking.
3. The defensive front alignment do not know who is receiving the football. The ball could be coming directly at them or could be handed off in the opposite direction.
4. The defensive team cannot go on fast pursuit to the ballcarrier due to the crossing movement in the offensive backfield.
5. Because of the action, the defensive secondary men may not key a man or ball. Rotation and other defensive stunts may not be able to be used. The defensive reactions to the offensive maneuvers will be slow also.
6. Defensive keying and reading may not be utilized, because the defenders do not know who is receiving the football.
7. Play action passes, reverses, bootlegs, etc., can easily be employed in the offensive sequence of plays.

Offensive Formations Utilized

There are a multitude of offensive formations the Cross-Buck sequence of plays can employ. Diagrams 9-2 through 9-4 illustrate a few of the sets that can be used. Any form of tight ends, split ends, flankers, slots, etc. can be utilized.

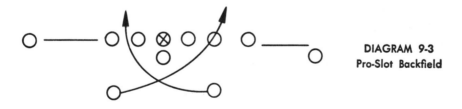

DIAGRAM 9-3
Pro-Slot Backfield

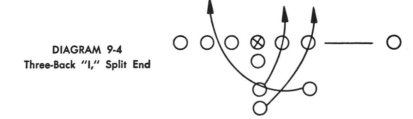

DIAGRAM 9-4
Three-Back "I," Split End

THE PLAY OF THE CROSS-BUCK

Since there are numerous Cross-Buck series utilized with different formations, not all plays and sets will be illustrated. However, almost all Cross-Buck sequences are similar in nature and in the purposes they attempt to accomplish. Diagram 9-5 indicates a Cross-Buck play with trap blocking utilized. The offense attempts to drive the fullback up the middle area to, *one,* hold the defensive middle defenders and, *two,* to plug the area where the offensive guard has left. From this one play, an entire series can be employed and exploited versus all defenses. The rules, execution and coaching points of every position is described with the Cross-Buck trap play.

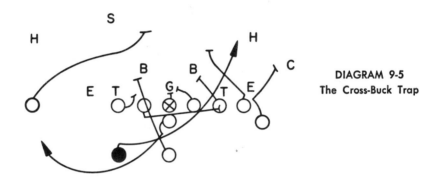

DIAGRAM 9-5
The Cross-Buck Trap

OFFENSIVE LINE

Onside End

Rule: Bump man over, block linebacker inside or pick up play.

Execution: On the snap of the ball, the end should fire-out block on the defender positioned over him. He should immediately release from the line of scrimmage and pick up the first linebacker aligned inside. If no linebacker is threatening, then he can block the first defender that shows. Go hard for the linebacker and put head in middle. Linebacker will be slow due to the execution in the backfield. Do not over-extend the body and go to the ground. Be in a good hitting position when driving for the linebacker.

Coaching Points: Keep the head up. Perform a bump maneuver on the defender positioned over. Keep a wide base and be quick going for the linebacker.

Onside Tackle

Rule: Block the first linebacker on or beyond the hole. Listen for "check" by guard to either "help" or "switch" assignments.

Execution: On the snap of the ball, the tackle should release to the inside and block the first linebacker that shows. He should be quick, but must not over-extend himself so that he goes to the ground. Stay low, keep head up and aim the head to chop defender down. If linebacker is positioned over, fire-out for man and put face into mid-section. Drive the linebacker off the line using short driving steps.

Coaching Points: Release hard and low. Do not over extend on the first step, because the linebacker is off the line of scrimmage. Put the head squarely in the middle of opponent and drive him out of the play.

Onside Guard

Rule: Over, inside—Make "check" call to tackle if double-team or step-around maneuver is desired.

Execution: If the defensive man is aligned over the offensive guard, he will explode from his offensive stance and execute a fire-out block on the defender. His head will be placed into the midsection of the opponent. The arms will come up and short driving steps will be utilized. The guard should not allow any penetration into the backfield. If blocking inside with a double-team on the defensive middle guard, the offensive guard should lead step down to the inside and aim his foot and head for the near hip of the defender. Once contact is made, he will slide his head to the outside and drive the man on a 45 degree angle off the line of scrimmage. If the defensive man is positioned in the gap, the offensive guard cannot allow any penetration. He must come down hard to the inside and aim his head for the far hip. Once penetration is prevented, then pursuit must be stopped.

Coaching Points: If defensive man is aligned over the offensive guard, he must stop pursuit action on his man. Screen the defender off by sliding head to the outside. Getting position on this man should be accomplished also.

Center

Rule: Number 0 man over, front-stack, backs over offside guard position.

Execution: On the snap of the ball, the center drives out hard for his opponent. First step should not be long, because a good snap must be executed first. A long lead step may cause a fumble. He should put face in the middle and slide his head to side of flow. If blocking back to offside guards position, he should lead step in that direction and should not allow penetration. Cut off pursuit.

Coaching Points: A proper snap and good exchange must be made with the quarterback. Step directly to the defensive man being blocked. Stay low, hit hard and come up through the man. Keep a wide base and use short driving steps to accomplish the job.

Offside Guard

Rule: Pull and block the first man beyond the guard's butt.

Execution: On the snap of the ball, the offside guard should take a short jab step back and down the line in order to get into his pulling lane. The head and arm should snap back hard in order to facilitate the pull maneuver. The body should not raise up, but should remain low to the ground. The next step is longer and the pulling guard begins to search out his blocking assignment. Once past the onside offensive guard his man will show. As he approaches defender he should shorten his stride, widen the base and begin to explode into the man. He should hit into the opponent and bring the arms up and through the man. Head should slide into the hole area.

Coaching Points: First step should not be long to over extend the body. Keep head up at all times. Run hard for defender before widening the base. Step and aiming point should be into the line of scrimmage. Block must be made from inside-out, not outside-in.

Offside Tackle

Rule: Seal-fire.

Execution: On the snap of the ball, the offside tackle should seal for the pulling guard. His first step should be a lead toward the puller. Do not allow any penetration by the defender. Attempt to get head across the body. Aiming point should be far hip. If no man comes, the tackle can fire up field for any defensive pursuit men.

Coaching Points: If no man is positioned over the offside guard, the tackle could seal inside and then come back on the defensive man aligned over him. Remain low to the ground and keep head up when performing the block. Tackle must be quick. Cut split down to the guard if block cannot be executed.

Offside End

Rule: Crossfield and block middle ⅓ of the defensive secondary.

Execution: On the snap of the ball, the offensive end releases from the line of scrimmage and sprints shallow to the line of scrimmage. He goes crossfield and blocks the middle ⅓ area. Do not look to the ballcarrier—he will find you.

Coaching Points: Look at the defensive man to be blocked and watch his eyes for the cut of the ballcarrier. Once the secondary defender makes his move, the end should throw a body block at him. Aim high for the face. Do not throw block far from opponent. Get close to man before block is executed.

OFFENSIVE BACKFIELD

Wingback

Rule: Fake on number 3, block number 4 man.

Execution: On the snap of the ball, the wingback executes a jab step inside faking a block on the number 3 defensive man. He pushes off his inside foot and blocks the number 4 man. He should remain low at all times.

Coaching Points: Screen the defensive man off from the play. Stay low, keep a wide base with the head up. Be in a good hitting position and explode into the opponent.

Quarterback

Execution: On the snap of the ball, the quarterback reverse pivots, gives a hand fake to the diving fullback and hands off to the halfback. He continues on a bootleg route after the exchange. He should read the defensive secondary for coverage.

Coaching Points: Reverse at 12 o'clock with the quarterback's back facing the offensive center. Pivot quick and do not stand up straight. Keep the ball into the stomach as the turn is executed.

Fullback

Execution: The fullback should take a lead step aiming for the offensive offside guard's position. He should drive straight ahead and take a fake from the quarterback. He must keep the head up and drive through the area as if he has the football. He should plug the area for any defensive stunts or men shooting the gap.

Coaching Points: The fullback must explode from his stance and be ready to strike anyone. He must stay low with knees running high. Be alert.

Tailback

Execution: On the snap of the ball, the tailback will take a short, quick jab step with his outside foot. On the next maneuver he will step behind the fullback's dive and receive an exchange with the quarterback. As he is given the football he should read the block by the pulling guard. He must cut off this block. Run for daylight.

Coaching Points: He should execute a good pocket for the quarterback with the inside elbow up. He must run hard and low to the hole.

The Fullback Dive

The fullback dive play can easily be added from the cross-buck trap just presented. In this instance, the quarterback hands the ball off to the fullback and fakes an exchange with the tailback. Diagrams 9-6 A and B illustrate regular and "I" formations with straight and step-around maneuvers. Diagrams 9-7 A and B indicate trap blocking versus even and odd defenses. Other blocking combinations can be utilized also.

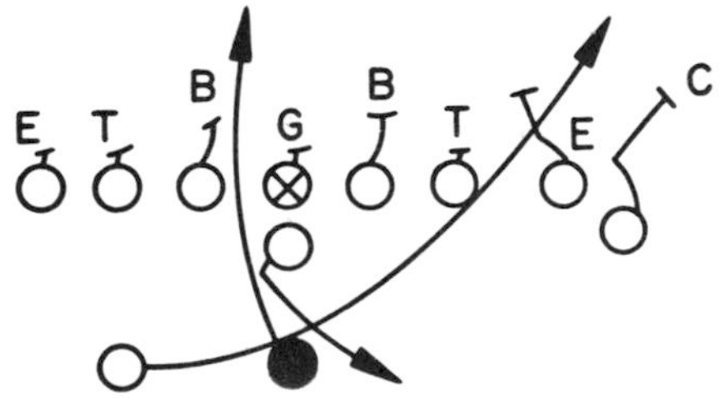

DIAGRAM 9-6A

DIAGRAM 9-6B

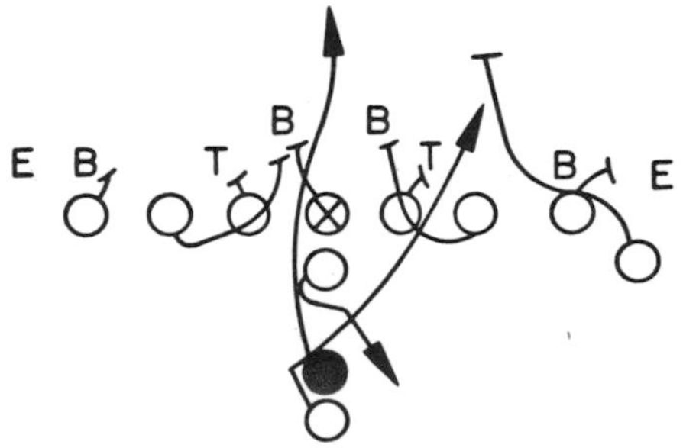

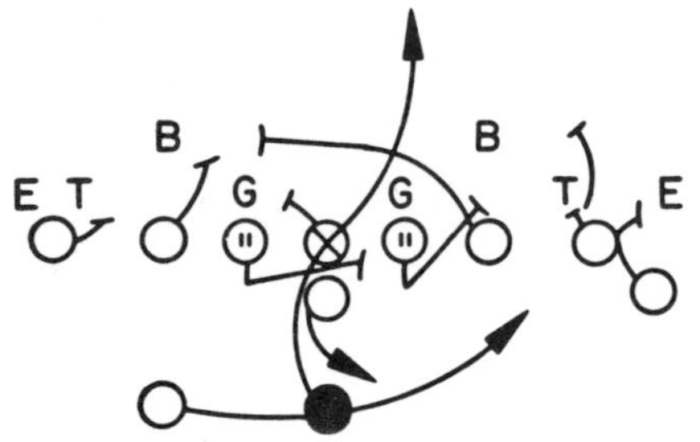

DIAGRAM 9-7A

DIAGRAM 9-7B

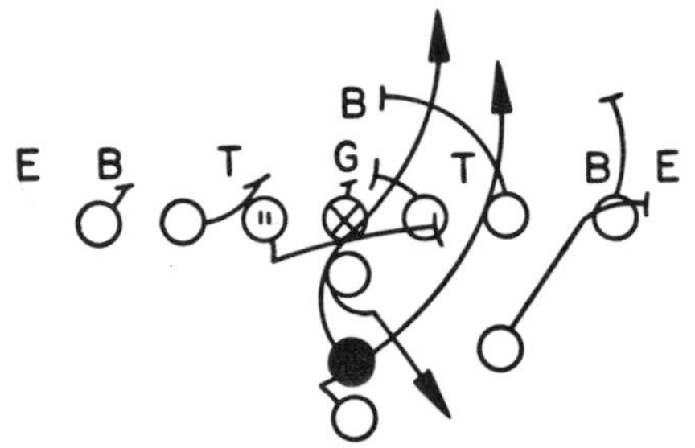

A tailback dive from an "I" formation can be accomplished also. Straight, cross, step-around and trap maneuvers can be employed. Diagram 9-8 shows a crossing action, similar to the fullback play, except the tailback receives the football.

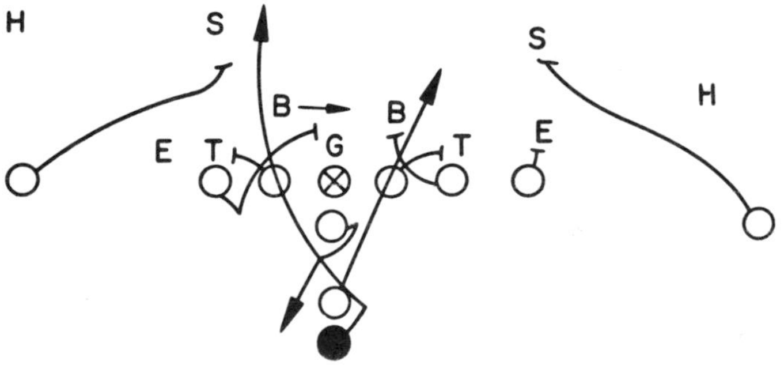

DIAGRAM 9-8

Power Sweep Cross-Buck

Power plays can easily be installed with cross action in the backfield. Diagram 9-9 indicates a power sweep with the onside halfback running in the opposite direction. The tight end and wingback double-team the defensive number 3 man while the onside offensive lineman utilize fire-out blocking techniques. The offside guard pulls and leads the play. The quarterback reverse pivots, gives a hand to the right halfback and exchanges the ball to the left tailback. The ball-carrier executes the power sweep play by lead stepping, crossing over and running the chalk line. He will key the block of the pulling guard.

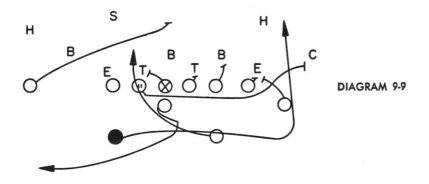

DIAGRAM 9-9

Power Off-Tackle Cross-Buck

The power off-tackle Cross-Buck is very similar to the sweep run. The same action occurs in the backfield (Diagram 9-10), except the tailback and guard aim at the off-tackle hole. One-on-one blocking can be used with the guard leading through the hole, or double-team blocking can be employed with the pulling guard trapping the defensive end (Diagram 9-11).

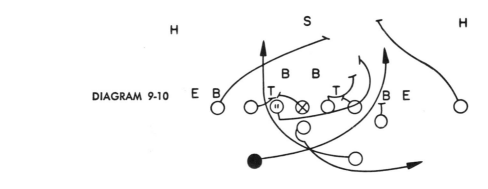

DIAGRAM 9-10

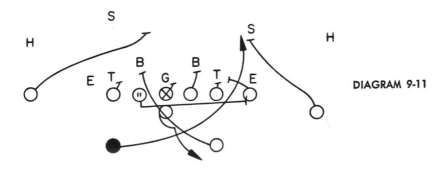

DIAGRAM 9-11

Three Back Cross-Bucks

Cross-Buck plays are excellent with the employment of three offensive backs. A great deal of faking and deception occur with these offensive sets. Diagrams 9-12 through 9-15 illustrate different Cross-Buck looks from the three-back "I" formation. Diagram 9-12 indicates the two "I" backs driving toward the strength of the formation, while the tailback crosses in the opposite direction. In Diagram 9-13, the fullback dives to the right, or weak side of the formation, while the deep "I" back drives to the strength. The strong tailback initiates a jab step to the outside and comes back in the opposite direction. Diagram 9-14 illustrates similar action, except the fullback runs to the strength and the tailback drives to the weak side of the set. Diagram 9-15 shows a Cross-Buck action with the fullback and left halfback, while the deep "I" back utilizes a jab step to the right and comes back toward the strength of the formation. Any offensive back can receive the football with the sequence of plays. Blocking on the line of scrimmage can differ from straight, cross, step-around and trap maneuvers.

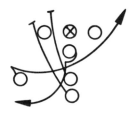

DIAGRAM 9-12

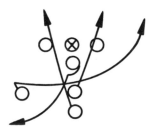

DIAGRAM 9-13

DIAGRAM 9-14

DIAGRAM 9-15

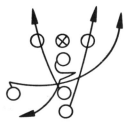

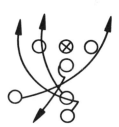

Cross-Buck Option

An excellent option play on any defensive end is a Cross-Buck action in the backfield with the quarterback coming down the line with the ball. This can be accomplished with three offensive backs. It is an excellent play, because it holds the defensive front alignment to the crossing backs and they cannot, therefore, react as quickly to the option (Diagram 9-16). The strength of the formation is to the right. The fullback dives right and the deep back runs left. The quarterback reverse pivots, fakes to both backs and comes down the line for the defensive end. The right halfback initiates a jab step outside and runs an option-pitch path parallel to the quarterback. He should stay approximately four yards deep and outside of the quarterback. The quarterback can either keep the ball and run or deliver the ball back to the halfback.

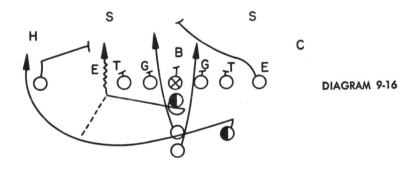

DIAGRAM 9-16

Cross-Buck Play Action Pass to Strength

Play action passes are necessary in all series. The cross-buck is no exception. All type of passes can be employed with any action used in the backfield. In Diagram 9-17 a play action pass is illustrated. It is similar to the Cross-Buck trap that was vividly described. The quarterback reverse pivots and fakes to both the diving fullback and the crossing tailback. He then sprints to the outside gaining depth in the backfield. He attempts to get outside the defensive end. If there is running room the quarterback should keep the football. However, if a receiver is open, he should try to pass to him. The wingback releases directly for a flag route while the tight end blocks one count and goes to the flat area. The offside end executes a trail pattern approximately 10 to 12 yards in depth. The onside lineman simulate a running play. Trap blocking is indicated, however, the pulling guard attempts to get outside the defensive tackle and stop any penetration and pursuit. The onside tackle pulls and attempts to hook the defensive end.

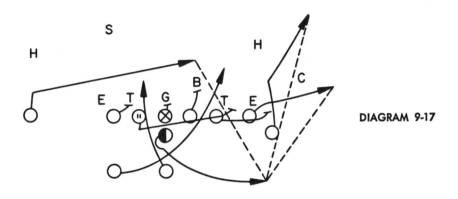

DIAGRAM 9-17

Cross-Buck Play Action Pass to the Weakside

Diagram 9-18 illustrates a play action pass from similar action previously mentioned, except the quarterback rolls to the opposite side. The fullback dives, slips through the line and sprints to the flat. The tailback crosses over and blocks. The split end executes a flag route while the tight end trails across field. The offside guard pulls and leads to protect the quarterback. The quarterback initiates fakes to the fullback and tailback respectively and runs to the weakside looking for any receiver that is open. He can run or pass the football.

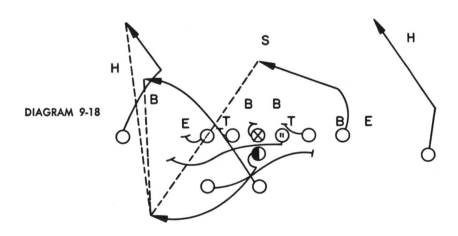

DIAGRAM 9-18

Drop-Back Passing

There are numerous and excellent passes that can be employed by the football coach. Any type of cross-action can be utilized in the backfield with the quarterback drop-back passing. The receivers can run any pattern necessary. Diagrams 9-19 through 9-22 illustrate different drop-back play action passes from crossing action in the backfield.

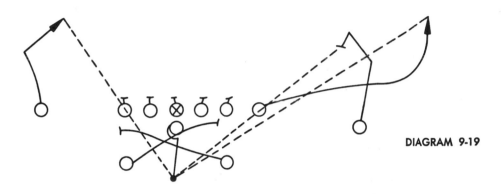

DIAGRAM 9-19

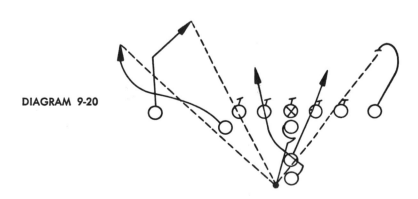

DIAGRAM 9-20

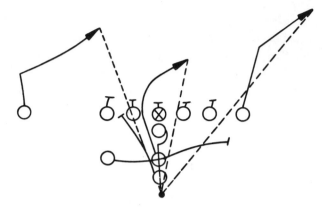

DIAGRAM 9-21

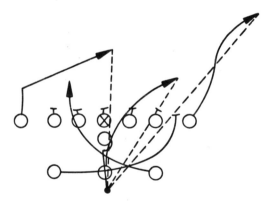

DIAGRAM 9-22

10

The Sprint-Out and Roll-Out
Passing Series

Today, the Sprint-Out or Roll-Out is one of the most potent attacks in high school and college. However, it is used sparingly at the professional level. The Sprint-Out pass employs one of three methods of attack. The play action pass from offensive running plays and the drop-back pass (Chapter 11) are other methods of attacking pass defense secondaries.

Attacking the Corner

The sprint-out pass (or roll-out) attempts to attack outside at the defensive corner or flat. It desires to put pressure in one specific area of the defensive alignment. In this case, it is the outside swing, short flat, medium outside, and deep outside areas. Intelligent and reliable pass patterns are used in attacking the defensive secondary coverages. Once the defense relieves pressure in these areas and resorts to defensive adjustments such as different rotations, looks, etc., the offense can attack other areas. This is done by either throwing back or running with the football at an offensive weakness that may have developed.

Pass Patterns and Routes

There are numerous philosophies as to the number of pass routes and patterns that should be utilized in the sprint-out. Some coaches use only a limited amount of patterns believing these routes will suffice. They believe that with few pass patterns, perfection will result. However, there are numerous coaches who utilize a multitude of pass routes and patterns to attack all secondary coverages and maneuvers. When any weaknesses result, the offense will be able to attack those weaknesses with the varied passing game. This can be done, because the protection remains similar on most patterns with only certain routes and cuts being altered. However, a multitude of patterns will result.

Reading and Keying in the Sprint-Out Pass

While reading and keying of the defensive linebackers and secondary has accomplished a great deal in the drop-back passing attack, there are coaches who utilize it in the sprint-out also. The offensive receivers are usually reading the movements of the defensive halfbacks and will run their pattern according to the maneuvers he executes. If any short pattern is run, the receivers will key the defensive linebackers flying back to their respective zones and the receivers will slide to the areas that are vacant. The quarterback will read the defensive secondary also. He must watch the receiver closely for the cut and route executed.

An example is illustrated in Diagrams 10-1A and B. The receiver, after the snap of the football, releases from the line of scrimmage and, on his approach move, reads the secondary. If rotation is utilized in the defensive secondary, the flanker will run a flag route away from the safety man and the flat zone area (Diagram 10-1A). However, if the halfback does not rotate up, but stays deep, then the flanker can execute an out cut (Diagram 10-1B). In this situation, the quarterback clears the center area and sprints to the outside. He reads the maneuvers of the defensive secondary halfback and the offensive receiver. As the receiver initiates his cut, the quarterback can deliver the football.

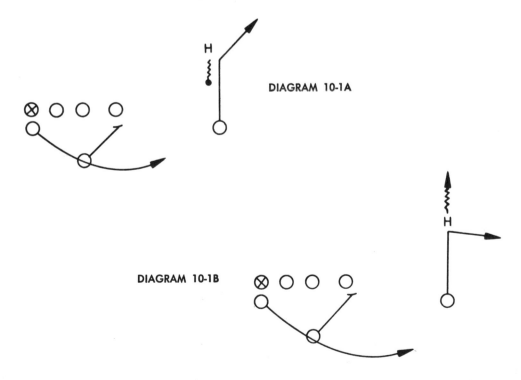

DIAGRAM 10-1A

DIAGRAM 10-1B

Another example is the keying of linebackers. Diagram 10-2 indicates the receiver executing a curl route and reading the outside linebacker. Once the linebacker makes his move, the receiver adjusts. The quarterback keys these movements and hits the open receiver in the vacant area also. The quarterback can read for "hot" receivers, which is explained in detail in Chapter 11.

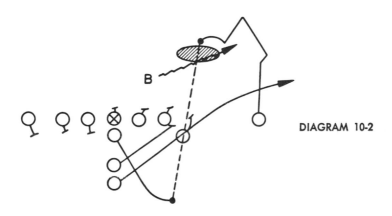

DIAGRAM 10-2

Most coaches, however, utilize general purpose passes to run versus most secondary coverages (man-to-man, zone, combination, etc.). The quarterback usually has one basic receiver as his first choice. If this man is covered, the quarterback usually will have second and third choices.

The Sprint-Out Versus the Roll-Out Pass

The sprint-out pass is executed with the step-out or face-out open step in the direction where the quarterback is going. If the quarterback is sprinting to the right, he will push off the medial side of the left foot and pivot the right foot in the direction of the route he is to execute. The step is short and "thrown out." On the first step the eyes focus on the receivers, while on the second, the ball must be in a ready position. The passer sprints to a position approximately 4 to 6 yards deep—the depth determined by the coach. When the quarterback reaches a position behind the end, he will immediately turn upfield toward the line of scrimmage. If a receiver is open, he will throw the ball quickly. If the passer finds that the receivers are covered, he will run the ball.

The roll-out pass is identical to the sprint-out, except the quarterback, when clearing from the center will execute a roll-out or reverse-pivot technique. If the play is going to the right, the quarterback must spin or pivot on the right foot. The left foot is brought up and around quickly, then planted in the desired direction. The ball is brought to the stomach, with the front of the body temporarily facing the direction opposite that of the intended line of flight. On the second step, the quarterback looks downfield to the receivers. On the third step he has the ball in "ready" position. If the quarterback false steps when clearing the center, the coach must insist he "fall away" from the center at a 45 degree angle in the direction of the roll. The roll-out may put the passer a little deeper into the backfield than the sprint-out.

Strengths and Advantages of the Sprint and Roll-Out Action

The strengths and advantages of sprinting out or rolling away from the center are as follows:

1. The sprint-out pass easily ties in with other plays (belly series, counters, bucks, etc.) of the offense.
2. It minimizes the danger of losing yardage. The passer is continually in motion toward the line of scrimmage.
3. All receivers in the pattern are in direct view of the passer.
4. It creates a very simple "read" for the passer. Through constant practice, he can develop proficiency regarding when to pass and when to run.
5. The possibility of a pass on every down causes the secondary men to freeze and hold their positions while deciding whether it is a pass or a run.
6. Persistent pressure is put on the corner man as to whether to defend against the run or pass.
7. Though the defense may apply internal pressure through the employment of shooting and stunting, the quarterback is constantly clearing away from the intended pressure.
8. Since half of the defensive linemen must chase farther for the passer, an extended rush is required, and this may exact a physical toll.
9. The offensive linemen have easier and better blocking assignments, since the defensive linemen have only one way to rush.
10. The defensive secondary must utilize different coverage whenever the ball is in a sprint-out or roll-out, causing additional problems for them.
11. With a fourth runner in the quarterback, the running attack is greatly expanded.

Semi-Sprint-Out and Semi-Roll-Out Pass

The execution of the semi-sprint-out pass begins the same as the sprint-out, except the quarterback will pull up either behind the end, tackle, or guard position. It is meant to look first like a sprint-out, but the quarterback stops and other patterns can be utilized by the receivers. It is also utilized to throw back across the field. The semi-roll-out pass clears the center the same as the roll-out and accomplished the same as the semi-sprint-out. The advantage of the semi-sprint-out and the semi-roll-out pass is that it can cause much confusion for the defensive secondary, deciding whether to rotate or not and whether or not it is a sprint-out-pass. It causes additional problems for the defensive linemen who have to chase to different positions instead of one as with the drop-back pass. The deeper pass can now be employed and the passer has more of a direct view of the entire playing field. Diagram 10-3 illustrates the quarterback routes in both the sprint, roll, semi-sprint, and semi-roll actions.

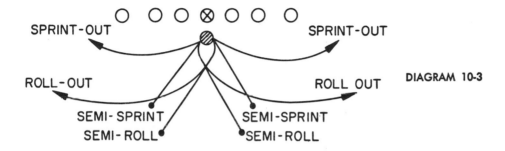

DIAGRAM 10-3

Formations Necessary

Almost any formation can be utilized in the sprint-out or roll-out pass. Usually some type of split end is good. A third quick receiver is usually best, such as a wingback or flanker.

THE PLAY OF THE SPRINT-OUT PASS

Diagram 10-4 indicates a Wing T and a split end with the sprint-out play shown versus the Split 4-4 defense. Diagram 10-5 illustrates the blocking versus six other defenses. The rules, executions, and coaching points follow.

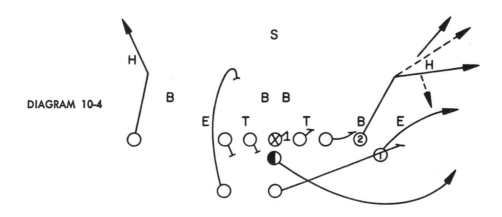

DIAGRAM 10-4

OFFENSIVE LINE

Tight End

Rule: Release and run the required pattern.

Execution: On the snap of the football, the tight end must release from the line of scrimmage and run for the outside leg of the defensive halfback. If the halfback retreats, the tight end will automatically do an out cut to the side line away from the floating opponent. However, if the halfback comes up as if to rotate, the tight end must execute a flag pattern attempting to outmaneuver the defensive safety man.

Coaching Points: Release hard and fast and sprint to a point about 10 yards before cutting. If bumped, get back on course. If the football is thrown, look the ball into the hands and be a runner. Catch the ball first before attempting to run.

Onside Tackle

Rule: Block the first offensive linemen on or outside.

Execution: On the snap of the football, the onside tackle must aim his head for the outside hip of his defensive opponent. He must take a lead step in that direction, place his head in and scramble block him. He should keep his hands and feet moving and attempt to cut the defender off.

Coaching Points: Must move quick to cut off opponent. Cannot go to the ground. Keep the head up with a wide base and back straight. Attempt to turn the man inside, if possible, and cut off any pursuit angles.

Onside Guard

Rule: Block the number 1 man.

Execution: The onside guard's primary job is similar to the offensive tackle. He must fire-out hard and low as to make the play look like a run. He should aim the head on the outside hip of the defensive opponent and attempt to scramble block him.

Coaching Points: The offensive guard must be quick and fast to stop any pursuit. He cannot go to the ground and should use his hands and feet to prevent falling.

Offensive Center

Rule: Block the number 0 man.

Execution: The offensive center's is similar to the offensive guard if covered. However, if he is not covered, he should drop back in a good cup position. He should keep a wide base, hips bent, back straight, bull the neck and keep the head up. The center should keep the feet moving and look for any off color jersey coming into his area. If no man shows, the center should immediately look to the outside and pick off any defensive rusher from that area.

Coaching Points: The center should stay low and move quick to pick off any rusher. He should either utilize a ride or a recoil method when hitting into the opponent. He should never ever extend himself and his hitting position. The center must keep the body and head in front of his defensive man so as to stop any pursuit by him to the quarterback. Chop the defensive opponent down if necessary.

Offside Guard

Rule: Block the number 1 man—cup protection.

Execution: On the snap of the football, the offside guard will take a step back and set up into a good cup blocking position. He must keep a wide base with the feet moving. The head is up, back is straight and the guard is ready to uncoil on his opponent. If no man comes into his area, he will immediately look to the outside for any defensive end rush.

Coaching Points: The offside guard must move quick and fast for his set up position. Do not cross the feet while moving. Keep the head and body in front of the opponent. Chop the defender down if necessary.

Offside Tackle

Rule: Block the number 2 defensive man—cup protection.

Execution: Same duties as the offside guard. If covered he will take his man. If no man on, look to the outside for defensive contain man.

Coaching Points: Same as offside guard's responsibilities.

Offside End

Rule: Release and run flag route.

Execution: On the snap of the football, the split end will release from the line of scrimmage, go hard for the defensive halfback, and execute a flag cut. The end should go hard and quick and not take it easy since the quarterback is going away. (The split end could execute a trail route with this pass for a safety valve also.)

Coaching Points: Read the secondary movements for coverage. If the defense is maneuvering a certain way, another pass pattern may be good. Alert the quarterback to this. Release hard, get even with the defender, have a good approach, and execute a good cut.

OFFENSIVE BACKFIELD

Wingback

Rule: Release to the flat.

Execution: On the snap of the football, the wingback will release right away to the flat area. On the second or third step he looks over his outside shoulder for the football. He should look quickly and not wait. The quarterback may throw the ball instantly, because of the defensive coverage and rush. Run at a 45 degree angle and get a depth of approximately three to four yards.

Coaching Points: Look the ball directly into the hands. Once the ball is caught get directly upfield and look for daylight. If ball is thrown to another receiver (tight end), help block for him.

Tailback

Rule: Run swing pattern.

Execution: The offensive tailback will release from his set position after the snap of the football and will execute a swing route approximately eight yards in depth. The tailback will key the linebacker in the area and will hook in or out and slide according to where this man is. If the linebacker goes inside, the tailback will hook outside and if the linebacker goes outside, the tailback will hook inside. Once the hook maneuver is accomplished, the tailback must slide inside or outside if the linebacker moves into his hook area.

Coaching Points: The tailback must release quick and get to the area right away. After hook route is executed, the tailback must come back toward the line of scrimmage and not move back into the linebackers or the defensive secondary. He should remain low to the ground and form a good pocket for the quarterback. While the quarterback will not throw back on this particular play, the tailback must execute this to hold the linebackers and defensive secondary.

Fullback

Rule: Block the first man outside the tackle's block.

Execution: On the snap of the football, the fullback will execute a lead step and aim for a point one foot wider than the tight end. He should take a course that is straight and should not execute a circled path. As he reaches the defensive end, the fullback should aim his head on the outside knee of the end and attempt to block him inside by getting an outside position and knocking him down. The fullback will keep his legs underneath him and should not throw the block quickly so as to lose his balance and go to the ground.

Coaching Points: The fullback should stay low and not run high at his opponent. The fullback cannot take a wider path to the defensive end for if he does, and the defensive end crashes hard to the inside, the fullback will not be able to block him. He should not go to the ground after the block has been executed, but should stay up and off the ground. Keep the body under control.

Quarterback

Execution: On the snap of the football, the quarterback will open-step in the direction of the sprint-out and come off the fullback's tail. The quarterback should get at a depth of approximately five yards and start to turn upfield once past the fullback's block. The ball should be brought up on the second step and be ready to be thrown on the third. He should key the fullback's block and look to the flat area immediately. The quarterback's main objective is to run the football. (Many coaches desire to pass first and run second.) However, if contain comes, then the quarterback should pass the football. He looks first at the wingback and second to the tight end. He should look for the tight end's cut off the defensive halfback's maneuver.

Coaching Points: Keep the ball up in the air at all times ready to pass it. Be ready to throw the ball on the third step especially if there is a quick rush by the defensive front alignment. Turn the shoulders square to the line of scrimmage when throwing the football. After the ball is released, point at the man throwing for a good follow-through technique.

The quarterback can reverse pivot on the quarterback action also. This is a roll-out maneuver which was explained previously. The same maneuvers by the offensive line and receivers is accomplished as was done in the sprint out.

The only difference in this method is the quarterback cannot see his receivers as quickly, because he is reverse pivoting away from the action on the first two steps. The ball must be brought quickly up to be able to throw instantly.

DIAGRAM 10-5

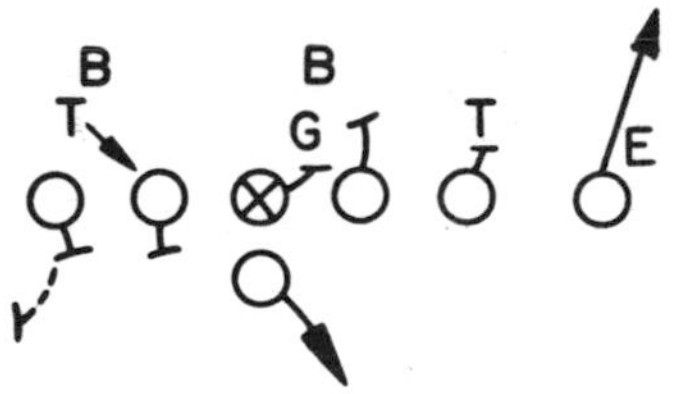

Versus 5-4 Stack

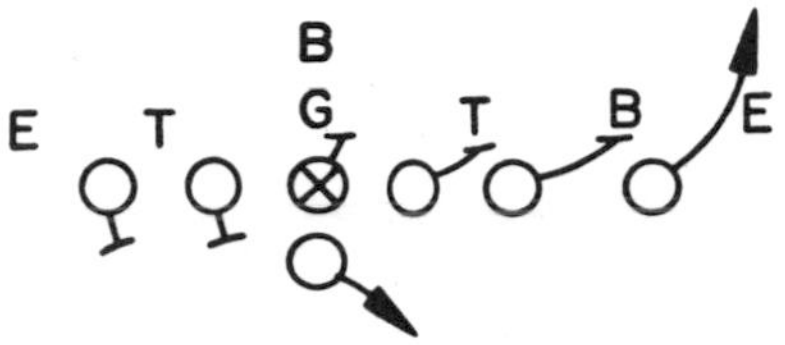

Versus 5-3

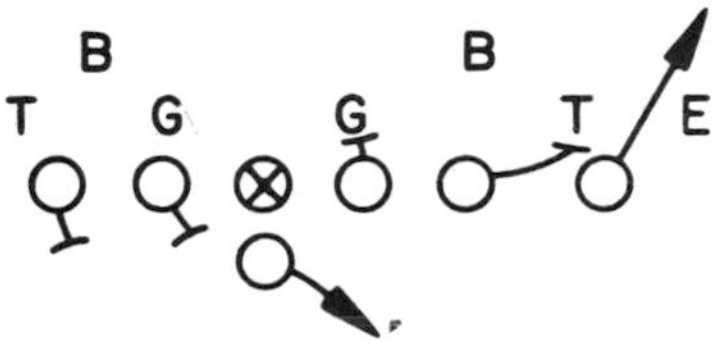

Versus Wide Tackle-6

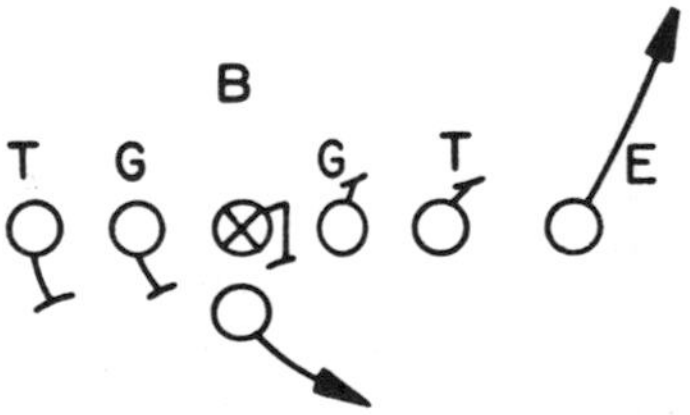

Versus 6-1

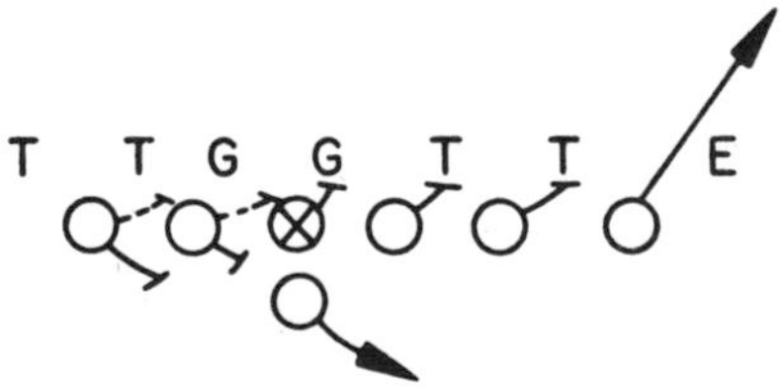

Versus Gap-8 Goalline

Versus 6-5 Goalline

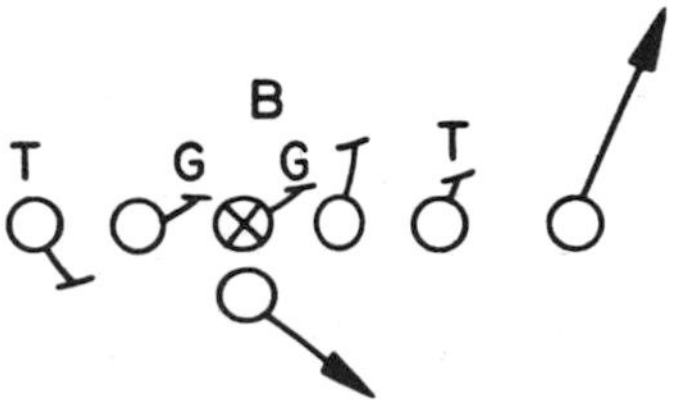

Other Blocking Combinations

In the sprint-out and roll-out pass, other blocking methods and combinations can be employed. Diagrams 10-6 and 10-7 illustrate reach blocking on the part of the offensive linemen. This is accomplished, because coaches believe the defensive front alignment cannot react as quickly to the fast sprint-out pass. Therefore, the offensive linemen reach for the next man over to stop any penetration. In some instances it adds another blocker to the outside, because the offensive tackle may be blocking on the contain such as versus a nine-man defensive front (5-4, 6-1, 4-3, etc.).

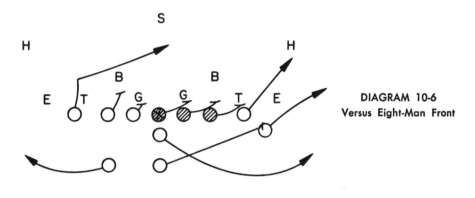

DIAGRAM 10-6
Versus Eight-Man Front

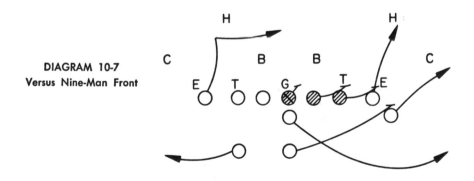

DIAGRAM 10-7
Versus Nine-Man Front

With any combination of blocking on the front side, the offside offensive linemen could fire-out instead of cup blocking as described. Again, the offside end could utilize a trail route or any other pattern necessary.

Area Blocking

If the offensive team is receiving a great deal of stunting and blitzing by the defensive team, the offensive line can revert to area blocking techniques. Each interior linemen will lead step in the direction of the sprint-out and look for any stunts in his area. If none occur, he will block his assignment. However, if any stunting does show, the offense can easily pick them up. The offensive linemen should remain low to the ground and must strike out at the opponents so as not to be "run over" by them. They must keep their bodies in front of their opponents. Diagram 10-8 illustrates the blocking methods versus three defenses and their stunting game.

DIAGRAM 10-8

Versus 5-4 Stunt

Versus Split-6 Stunt

Versus 6-1 Stunt

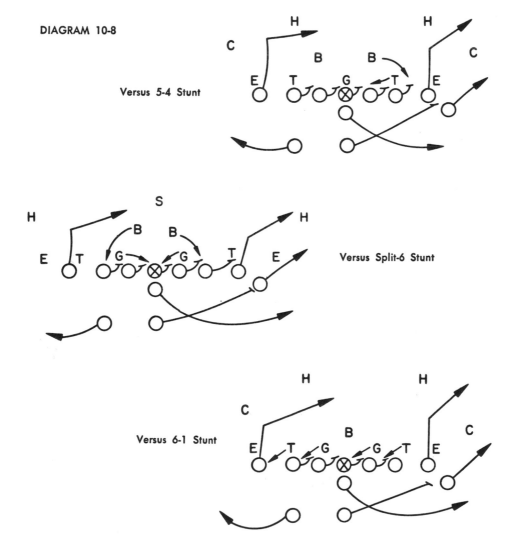

The Sprint-Out Pass to the Split End

The sprint-out or roll-out pass can easily be executed to the split end side also (Diagram 10-9). In this case, the tailback sprints to the flat and looks over his outside shoulder for the ball. The split end will run a flag route and/or key the movement of the defensive halfback. The tight end will run a hook pattern and key the linebackers while the wing runs an out and up streak route. The quarterback and fullback coordinate together, as was accomplished to the tight end side. Diagram 10-10 indicates a sprint action to a slot formation.

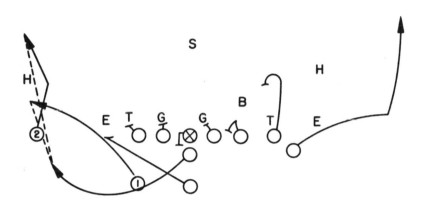

DIAGRAM 10-9

DIAGRAM 10-10

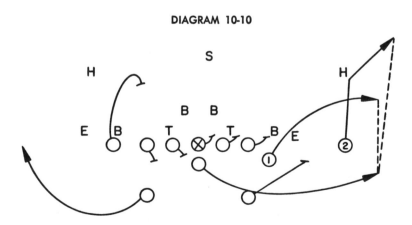

Sprint Action with the Tight End to the Flat

Another pass pattern that can be utilized is to send the tight end to the flat and put the wingback on a flag route (Diagram 10-11). All other assignments and responsibilities remain the same. The quarterback attempts to hit the tight end first and the wingback second.

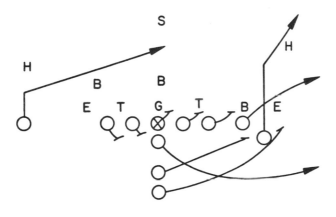

DIAGRAM 10-11

Semi-Sprint Pass Patterns to the Onside

There can be numerous pass patterns employed by the offensive coach when utilizing semi-sprint or semi-roll action. The team can utilize basic patterns, flood a certain zone or area, employ crossing action, use delay type passes, etc. The best utilization to the onside for semi-sprint-out is the use of a wide flanker or slot set. More pass routes can then be utilized to the onside. Diagram 10-12 illustrates a wing formation with the tight end going to the flag while the wingback starts outside, but climbs the hash mark. The quarterback rolls behind the guard-tackle seam and looks for the open receiver. It must be remembered that with the semi-sprint or semi-roll the quarterback can throw longer and deeper to his receivers. Also, the offensive linemen will have to use different pass blocking techniques. They must block higher and harder for the defensive rushers have less distance to rush. It is important that the offensive linemen know exactly where the quarterback is setting so they will know where to block their opponents away from the area.

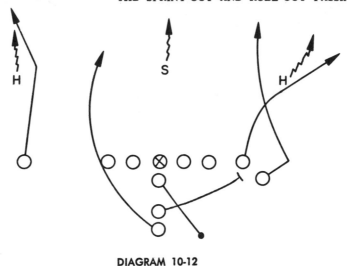

DIAGRAM 10-12

Diagrams 10-13 through 10-18 illustrate a few pass patterns that can be utilized to the onside with slot and flanker formations. Diagrams 10-19 through 10-25 indicate other schemes with three men releasing to the onside. The quarterback, in all cases, must know his primary and secondary receivers. If none are open, he should run with the football. He should set up behind the guard or tackle approximately seven to eight yards in depth. The offensive linemen's blocking combinations and patterns remain similar on all pass routes.

DIAGRAM 10-13
The Curl Pattern

The quarterback looks wide then scans to the tight end first and flanker second.

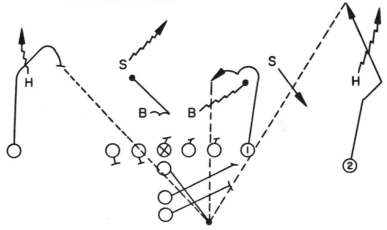

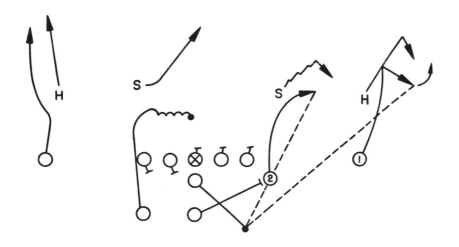

DIAGRAM 10-14
The Sideline Pattern

The quarterback will look to the split end first. This is good
if safety is covering slot or split end is double covered.

DIAGRAM 10-15
Double Post Pattern

Flanker is number one receiver. Slot attempts to occupy
safety and tight end does the same with the halfback.

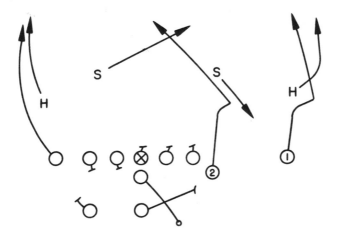

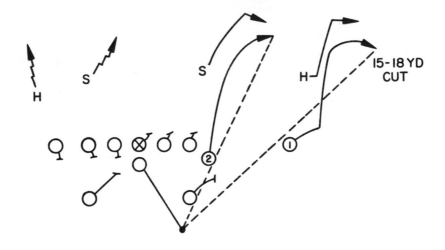

DIAGRAM 10-16
The Out Pattern

This is a 15-18 yard pattern. The split end comes back to the sideline and the quarterback gets deeper for a longer pass.

DIAGRAM 10-17
The Sideline and Go Pattern

Everyone blocks on this play. The ball can be thrown at 5 yards, but if covered tight, the ball is thrown deep.

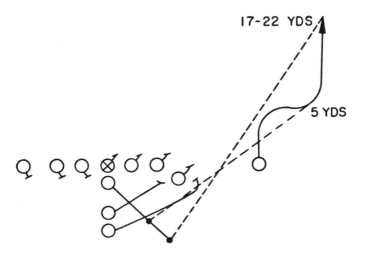

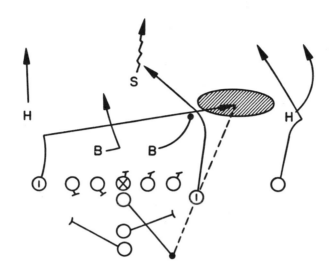

DIAGRAM 10-18
The Drag Pattern

DIAGRAM 10-19
The Pick Pattern

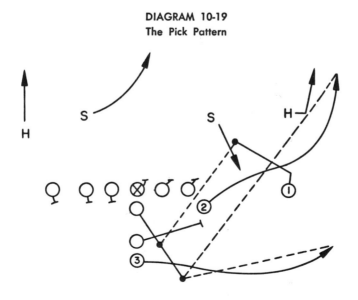

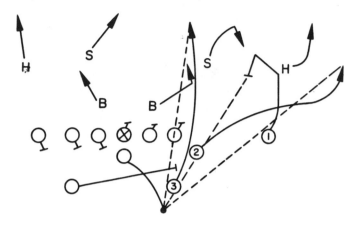

DIAGRAM 10-20
The Curl Pattern

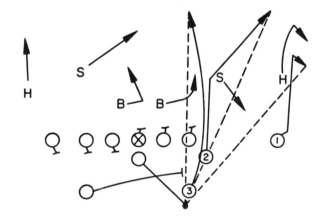

DIAGRAM 10-21
The Square-Out

DIAGRAM 10-22
The Shoot Pattern

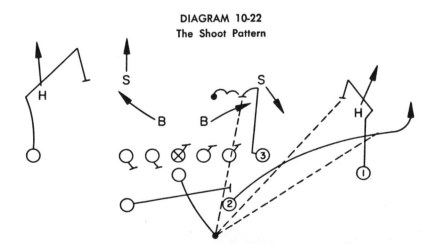

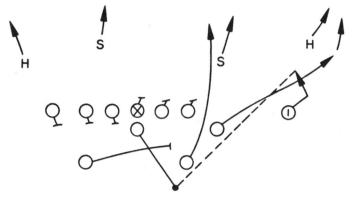

DIAGRAM 10-23
The Delay Pattern

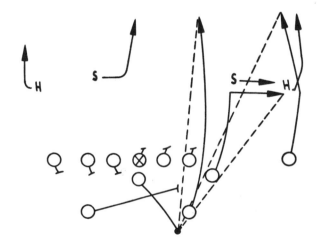

DIAGRAM 10-24
The Wrinkle Pattern

DIAGRAM 10-25
The Snake Pattern

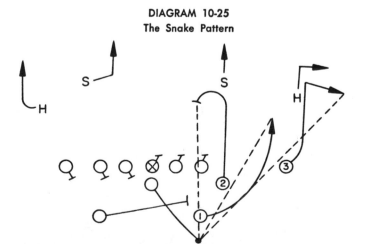

The Throw Back Patterns

From the semi-sprint and semi-roll action, throw-back pass patterns can easily be accomplished. The offensive team should throw back when it finds the defensive secondary coverages tightening to the onside, such as employing some form of rotation or combination zone and man-to-man. Diagrams 10-26 through 10-30 illustrate throw-back patterns and schemes with different sets and formations. A multitude of the patterns and cuts can easily be done from many different formations and looks.

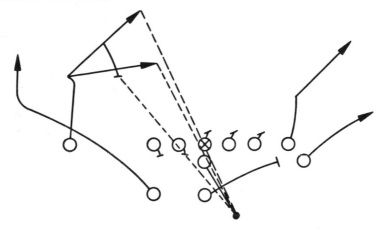

DIAGRAM 10-26
"Split End Curl, Drag, Post, Streak"
Throw back to split end.

DIAGRAM 10-27
"Tight End Hook, Drag, Post, Streak"
Throw back to tight end.

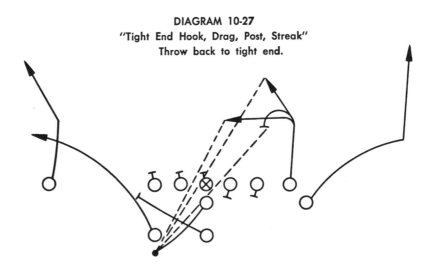

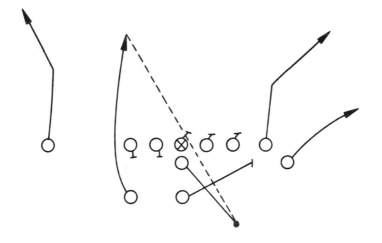

DIAGRAM 10-28
Throw-Back Deep to Tailback

DIAGRAM 10-29
Throw-Back to Tight End from Slot Formation

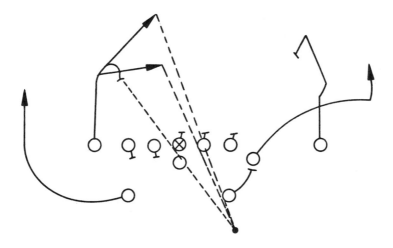

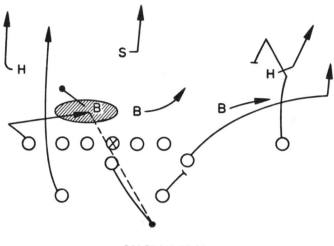

DIAGRAM 10-30
Throw-Back Delay

Tight end blocks and delays two counts, then runs to vacant
area.

Draws, Screens, and Roll-Back Passes

From the sprint-out passing game there must be other methods of attacking the defensive team, especially when they are prepared for the pass or anticipate it. Draws, screens and roll-back passes to confuse the defensive secondary and front alignment are excellent techniques to employ. Diagram 10-31 illustrates a middle draw, and Diagrams 10-32 and 10-33 indicate outside draws from the sprint-out look. Diagram 10-34 shows a middle screen, while Diagrams 10-35 and 10-36 indicate outside screens. Diagram 10-37 illustrates a roll-back pass with the defensive secondary rotating in one direction and the quarterback going in the other.

DIAGRAM 10-31
A Middle Draw

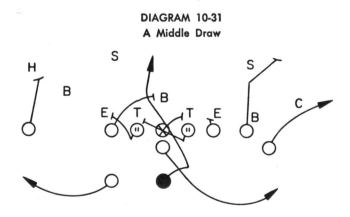

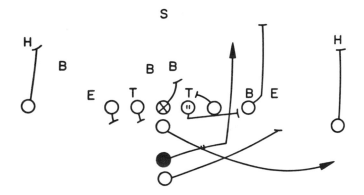

DIAGRAM 10-32
An Off-Tackle Draw

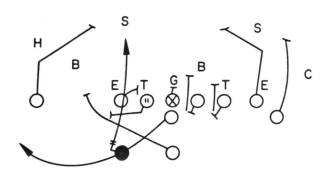

DIAGRAM 10-33
Tailback Off-Tackle Draw

DIAGRAM 10-34
Middle Screen

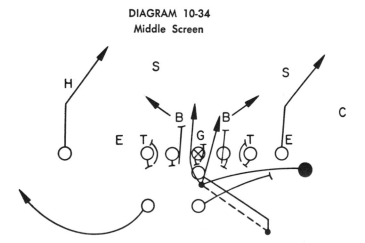

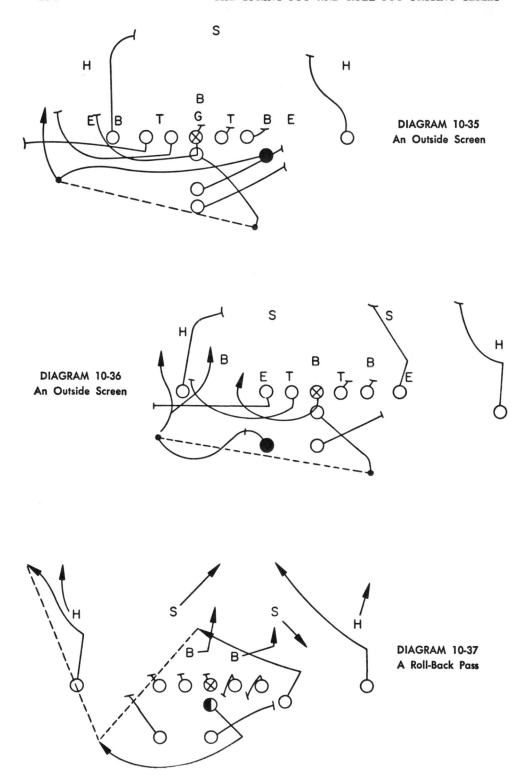

DIAGRAM 10-35
An Outside Screen

DIAGRAM 10-36
An Outside Screen

DIAGRAM 10-37
A Roll-Back Pass

11

The Drop-Back Passing Series

The Drop-Back passing game is employed to a great extent in professional football. At the college level, Drop-Back passing is used by a number of teams but not to the degree of the professional organizations. In high school, the Drop-Back passing game is utilized to a limited extent, because of the quarterback situation. However, there are numerous high schools that do utilize the Drop-Back pass successfully. There is a great deal of difference in the type of Drop-Back pass employed also. In most instances, especially at the high school and college level, reading and keying of the defensive linebackers and secondary is not accomplished. Pass routes and patterns are designated with primary and secondary receivers. The quarterback drops back and looks to his first receiver. If he is not open, the quarterback scans for the secondary man. However, a few colleges across the nation and entirely all the professional teams employ reads and keys by the quarterback before and after the snap of the football. The receivers are keying secondary people and linebackers for different defensive coverages and maneuvers also. Offensive backs are taught to key linebackers and defensive secondary men. Each offensive man (quarterback, flanker, split end, and backs) coordinate together on all pass routes and cuts. Each man's move is dependent upon the direction of the defensive secondary and linebackers after the snap of the football. It is desired that strategy with intelligent thinking by the offense will outmaneuver the opponent more than brute force will accomplish.

The Passing Game

The ingredients of a good passing game are important. The protection, receivers, quarterback, coverage, and strategy are all necessary in the Drop-Back passing attack. The football coach should know the number of pass patterns and cuts he desires to install. The quarterback should know how to attack certain personnel of the opponent and understand the rules in avoiding interceptions, etc. The coach and quarterback should realize the areas of the field to attack such as the short flats and short middle, the medium outsides and medium mid-dle, and the deep outsides and deep middle. Other areas include the outside swing and middle shuffle areas. The passing tree is necessary also. Every route and pass cut are necessary such as the quick out, hitch, slant, hook, hook and out, drag-in, square-out, sideline, go and out, comeback, post, streak, flag, etc., are needed for the wideout people. Flare, swing, flat, flag and post routes, etc., for the setbacks must be taught, drilled and practiced continually if a passing attack is going to be successful.

Reading, Keying, and Controlling in the Drop-Back Passing Game

There are basically two ways to attack a defensive weakness; *before* the snap of the football, and *after* the snap of the football. This is done by the quarter-back to get the best pass route and cut in the weakest area of the defense due to its coverage. This is accomplished in order to get a completion, cut down on mistakes, avoid interceptions, and have the best passing *percentages* versus the defensive team. For an example, if the flat areas are uncovered completely, the offense can attack that area with eight- and ten-yard pass cuts with out, hook, hook and out, etc., maneuvers. Reading is accomplished *before* the snap of the football. Blocking on the line of scrimmage is maximum with the offensive line and backs, because with no defensive men stationed in the flat areas to either side more stunting, red dogging, and blitzing can occur. The quarterback there-fore, comes up to the line of scrimmage, looks to see which wide out will be open and attempts to hit the receiver.

However, once the defensive team begins to cover the areas on the football field, such as the flat areas, the offensive team can read and key *after* the snap of the football for the maneuvers of the defense. The defensive team will usually have less people to stunt and blitz and, therefore, more people (offensive backs) can release in the secondary.

With the drop-back pass, the offensive team believes it can *control* the movements of the defense. If the defense does one maneuver, the offensive peo-ple will do another. The offense, therefore, controls the football game or its op-ponent. It believes the percentages are there that a better pattern will be run versus the secondary coverages employed. Pass routes and cuts called will change if the defensive team utilizes another coverage.

Strategy plays an important role in the development of the passing pattern. The coach should know, through the utilization of films, scouting and observa-tion the movements of the defensive team. Once these are known and studied, the coach can employ passing cuts and maneuvers versus these coverages. Dur-ing the week of the game, the quarterback, receivers, backs, and interior linemen will work and drill versus the movements of the defense.

COACHES BELIEFS IN THE DROP-BACK PASSING GAME

There are numerous coaches in the passing attack that believe a defensive team must cover the eight areas on the field (the four deep and the four short areas) and use a three man rush only to do an effective job versus the drop-back pass. These coaches believe that if the defensive team does not cover one of these areas the quarterback and receivers will coordinate to attack it before the defense can pull the quarterback down. Even if the defensive team has more rushers than the offense has protectors the quarterback should get the ball to the open receivers quick. It must be remembered, however, it is the coach who has "the chalk last" that wins. A great deal of strategy can be accomplished, but the offensive team must be able to accomplish these feats versus the many defensive maneuvers and coverages.

READING THE MIDDLE LINEBACKER OR "MIKE"

In most pass patterns called and designated the quarterback and tight end read the movements of the defensive middle linebacker or "mike" man. Every defense has a "mike" linebacker whether he is a middle linebacker or not. Diagram 11-1 (pp. 195–6) shows three defenses with the "mike" indicated. "Mike"

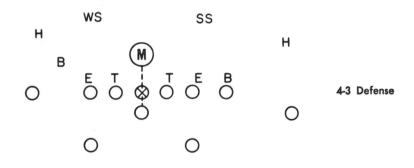

DIAGRAM 11-1

Quarterback must read "mike" linebacker.

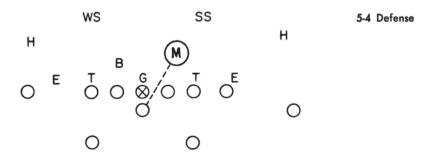

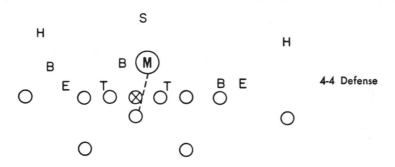

is considered to be the first linebacker located over the center or first linebacker out toward the tight end. As the ball is centered, the quarterback retreats for the required depth, and reads the movements of the "mike." If he comes "forward" or "vacates," the quarterback will flip the ball to the tight end or any other "hot" receiver. However, if he is covered, he will *not* throw the football. The tight end, at the same time, is reading "mike" also. He will look for the football if the linebacker does any of the two maneuvers mentioned (Diagram 11-2). The tight end's release will be dependent upon the play of the defense and its secondary coverage. If the defensive secondary is four deep, the tight end will release in-

DIAGRAM 11-2

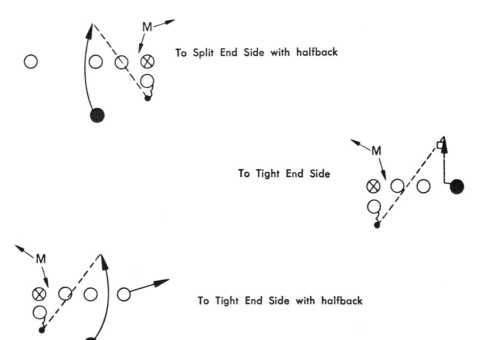

side. However, if the defense is a three deep diamond secondary, the tight end will usually release outside (Diagram 11-3). Both the tight end and quarterback must work and coordinate together for this quick pass. The quarterback must toss the ball quickly, with force, and over the heads of the oncoming defensive rushers. The tight end can yell "hot," however, this is not always necessary.

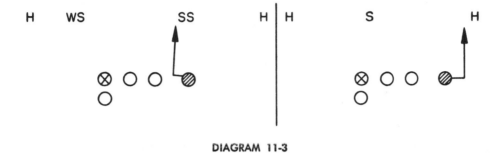

DIAGRAM 11-3

OUTSIDE LINEBACKER READ BY THE QUARTERBACK

There are only a few schools that look to the outside linebacker for the next read. The quarterback, after keying the middle linebacker, retreats and looks to the outside linebacker for coverage. Whether it be to the split end or flanker side, the quarterback watches the coverage (man to man or some type of zone in the flat, curl, or hook area) or rush. Once this read is accomplished by the quarterback, he will throw or look to another area on the field. For an example, if the call was toward the flanker side and the mike went toward the hot receiver, the quarterback then scans the coverage to the outside. If the tight end is covered tight by the outside linebacker such as on man to man, the quarterback could hit the halfback out in the flat area (Diagram 11-4). Many other patterns and pass cuts could be made also.

DIAGRAM 11-4

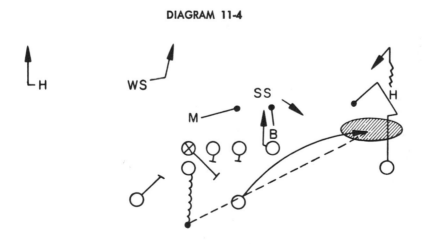

STRONG SIDE SAFETY READ FROM A 4-DEEP SECONDARY

From the outside linebacker read the quarterback looks quickly to the strong side safety. Coaches who do not utilize the outside linebacker key go from the mike read to the strongside safety automatically. The quarterback reads the movements of the strongside safety and will pass the ball according to his movements. An example of reading and keying by the quarterback and other offensive people is illustrated in Diagram 11-5. The quarterback calls for

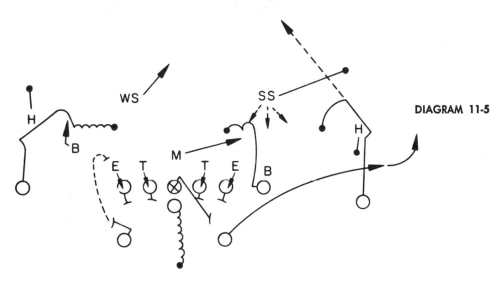

DIAGRAM 11-5

a pattern to the flanker side as shown. The tight end releases inside, because of the four deep secondary, and reads the "mike" linebacker. Since the mike does not stunt or vacate, the tight end continues on his route and hooks in the area indicated. Once the hook maneuver is accomplished, the tight end reads the linebacker again for coverage and slides inside if mike goes outside, etc. The flanker releases from the line of scrimmage and reads the movements of the strongside safety man. If this defender retreats in any direction, the flanker will run his curl route. However, if the strongside safety comes up in any manner, the flanker will adjust the route and go on a post maneuver attempting to stay away from the weakside safety man filling that area. The offensive halfback reads the defensive halfback's maneuver. If the defensive halfback retreats, the offensive halfback will stay near the line of scrimmage. However, if the defensive halfback comes up as indicated, the halfback will gain yardage into the defensive secondary. This is done, because as the defensive halfback retreats, he will have a longer distance to take if the ball is thrown to the offensive halfback in the flat area. However, if he comes forward the offensive back will sprint for depth and when the proper instant arrives will climb the sideline attempting to out run the defensive halfback. The left halfback will block. However, if he sees no man is threatening the quarterback and the offensive linemen do not need assistance, the halfback can "sneak" out into a vacant area of the defensive secondary as shown. The split end releases and runs a curl maneuver. He reads the movements of the outside weak linebacker and will slide according to the movements of this defender.

The quarterback takes the snap from center and reads the mike linebacker first. If the linebacker does not come or vacate, he will not throw the quick pass to the hot receiver. The quarterback then continues to get depth and reads the strongside safety. The quarterback looks to the flanker for the curl as his primary receiver. If he is open, the quarterback should pass to him. The next man to hit is the halfback in the flat and the third is the tight end. If the flanker adjusts his route to the post, because of the safety man's movement, the quarterback should attempt to pass the ball to him immediately. Once the quarterback scans the onside and finds all receivers are covered, he should look to the other side for the split end curling and sliding or the left halfback on another pattern if he desires to release.

Another example of a read and key is illustrated in Diagram 11-6. The tight end releases and keys the strongside safety. If the safety goes to the flat or deep outside for zone coverage, the tight end will curl outside. However, if the safety plays man to man, the tight end will run an out route to the sideline. Again, the quarterback reads the mike, then strong safety, and passes the ball according to the route run and which receiver is open. He scans the field from right to left.

DIAGRAM 11-6

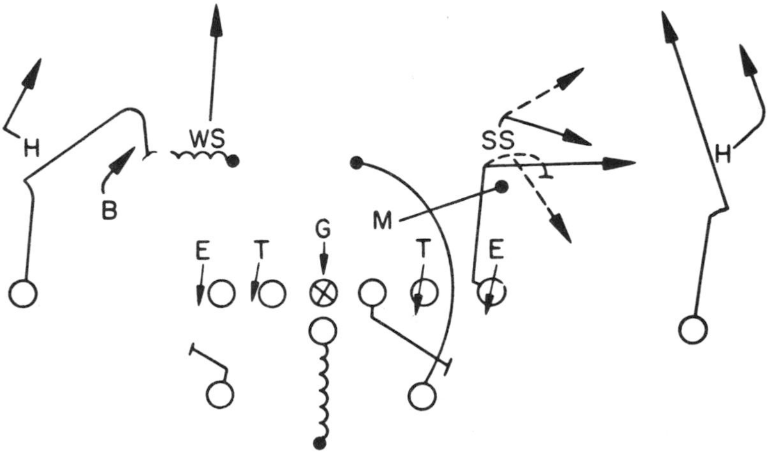

Different reads and keys can be accomplished to the split end side also. In all cases, the quarterback and receivers are attempting to control the movements of the defensive secondary and linebackers according to its coverage *after* the snap of the football. Every receiver and blocker have their keys and reads and each one must coordinate on their routes, cuts, and blocks. The quarterback must read and key the mike and strongside safety. The offensive backs must key their respective linebackers for blocking purposes and look to the defensive linebackers and halfbacks for the type of route executed. Each receiver must key the linebackers after the cut has been made for inside and outside sliding, etc. All must coordinate to do the proper job necessary for success.

THE USE OF OFFENSIVE BACKS FOR KEYING PURPOSES

In many cases, the utilization of the offensive backfield can be invaluable to the football coach. The defensive secondary and linebackers at times key the offensive backs for possible defensive rotation and coverage. If the backs split, flow to strength, flow away from strength, or cross (Diagram 11-7), the

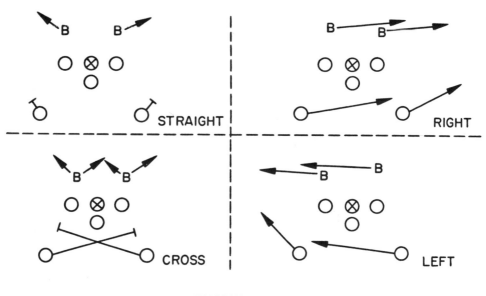

DIAGRAM 11-7

linebackers or secondary people may react in a certain direction. If this is accomplished, it is important for the coach and quarterback to spot this and run routes and patterns according to what is being executed by the defensive team. Films, scouting and observation should help a great deal in this venture.

TIMING IS ESSENTIAL

It is important that the quarterback release the football within a given amount of time. Usually 3.5 to 4 seconds is good. With any more time the offensive protection could break down. Depending upon speed, it should take the quarterback approximately 1.5 seconds to get the required depth and 1 second to make up his mind on who should receive the ball. The receiver should take so many seconds to run his pattern (usually 2.2 seconds). The quarterback and receiver should time the pass and route so as to coordinate.

OFFENSIVE SPLIT

Splitting on part of the offensive line, flanker, split end, and backs are important versus different defenses and their secondary coverages. Versus a three deep, for an example, the split end and flanker may desire to take maximum splits to widen the three deep defenders. However, versus a four deep, this may not want to be executed. Different areas on the field and pass routes will determine, in many cases, the splits and adjustments that must be accomplished.

NUMEROUS MISTAKES CAN OCCUR

With the reading and keying of the defensive front alignment and secondary, a great deal of mistakes can easily occur. The flanker, tight end, split end, offensive backs, and quarterback must coordinate together and make their correct cuts if the offensive team is to be successful. Drilling and practice time is of the utmost importance. If the football coach does not have essential time he may desire not to read and key versus the defensive opponent.

FLARE CONTROL

Many teams that utilize the drop-back passing attack, but do read or key, employ offensive backs to release. Coaches hope by doing this they will control linebackers or underneath coverage so that the primary receiver (flanker, end, etc.) will be open. This can be accomplished quite easily according to the pattern and route used. This is known as "flare control."

Primary and Secondary Choices

As just mentioned, the quarterback does not have to read the defensive secondary. The coach can implement different pass patterns and have the quarterback drop-back and pick out his primary and secondary receivers. Keying of the middle linebacker, outside linebacker and strongside safety does not have to be accomplished. Many coaches utilize this method which is much easier and simpler.

Strengths and Advantages of the Drop-Back Pass

The strengths and advantages of the drop-back passing attack are as follows:

1. A passer who has limited ability as a runner, but is a great passer, can utilize the drop-back pass to an enormous extent.
2. A passer can view the entire field from the drop-back position and can pass to both sides of the formation equally well.
3. The drop-back pass makes great use of the screen, draws, swing passes, and delay passes.
4. If the offense is widened and spread, the receivers can release easier and the widening helps isolate the receivers on the defenders.
5. This widening usually forces a one-on-one situation with the defensive secondary, which makes it easier to complete passes.
6. The deep pass or long ball can be thrown simply from the drop-back pass.
7. The passer can easily read the defense and hit the open receiver with accuracy.
8. The protection knows exactly where the passer sets up to pass the ball and will attempt to force the rushers to the outside.

Formations Employed with the Drop-Back Passing Attack

There are a multitude of formations that can be implemented with the passing attack. Usually wide-out people are the best and this should be accomplished to either side of the formation. An offensive back should be in the position to get into the passing lanes also. This is accomplished from an offensive halfback's position. Diagram 11-8 illustrates three different formations that can be used by the offensive team.

DIAGRAM 11-8

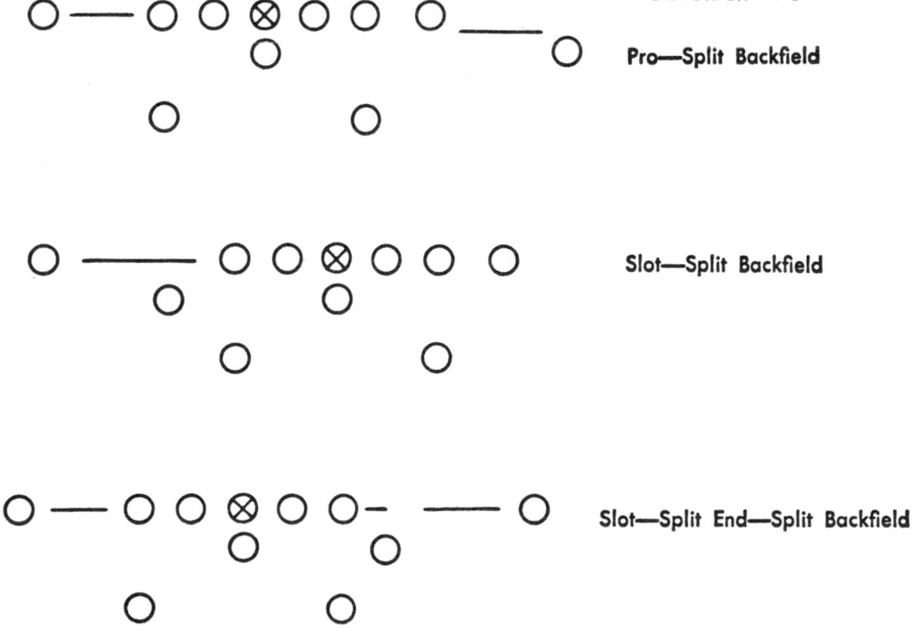

Pro—Split Backfield

Slot—Split Backfield

Slot—Split End—Split Backfield

Protecting the Passer

There are numerous methods to protect the passer in the drop-back passing series. The three methods basically utilized are as follows:

1. Man on Man Blocking
2. Linemen on Linemen Blocking
3. Cup Blocking

MAN ON MAN BLOCKING

Man on man blocking requires that the offensive linemen covered by defensive linemen will block these men. The theory behind this is "big men on big men." The uncovered linemen will listen for the offensive flow in the backfield and which back is to block, release, or both. The offensive backs that block look to the linebackers first. In this instance, therefore, the uncovered offensive linemen will pull automatically and help block outside once a back is directly assigned a linebacker. If, however, the quarterback has the offensive backs release, the uncovered linemen check for any stunts or blitzes first by the linebackers, and pull out to block any outside rushers. Diagrams 11-9A, B, and C illustrate these maneuvers. Any offensive route can be executed by the releasing back. The offensive linemen must know, however, the direction of the

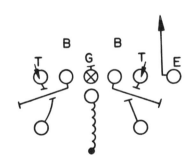

DIAGRAM 11-9A
Backs Blocking

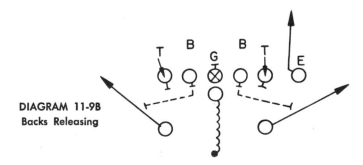

DIAGRAM 11-9B
Backs Releasing

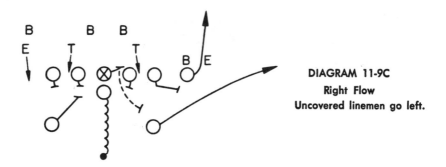

DIAGRAM 11-9C
Right Flow
Uncovered linemen go left.

backfield flow. When this is known, the uncovered linemen block opposite the flow. Three examples are shown in Diagram 11-10. Of course, the quarterback must designate the formation, flow of offensive backs, and who is to release or block. This alerts the offensive linemen if they must stay in and check first or pull directly out for outside rushers. If the backs who are assigned to block find their assignments not rushing, these men can run complimentary pass routes.

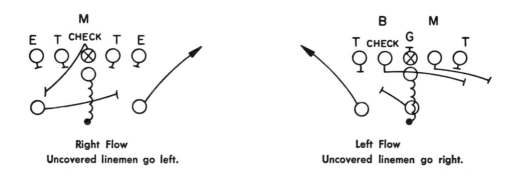

Right Flow
Uncovered linemen go left.

Left Flow
Uncovered linemen go right.

Split Flow or Cross Flow
Uncovered linemen go left.

DIAGRAM 11-10

LINEMAN ON LINEMAN BLOCKING

Another good method for protecting the passer is for the backs to step at the linebackers and block them wherever they fire or blitz. The offensive linemen never block linebackers. If the linebackers do not penetrate, the backs will assist the linemen with their blocks or release on a pass route. The center takes the man over him if he comes; otherwise, he should help to one side or the other. The guards block the first man down the line. The tackles block the second man down the line. The advantage of this blocking and that of man to man is that the smaller offensive back can usually block the smaller linebacker better than he can block the bigger end. The guards and tackles will now be blocking the bigger defensive linemen (Diagrams 11-11 and 11-12).

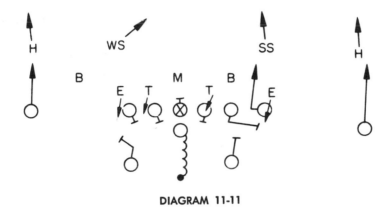

DIAGRAM 11-11

DIAGRAM 11-12

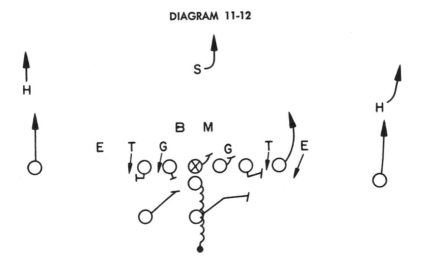

CUP BLOCKING

Cup blocking requires the five interior linemen to protect the inside (forcing the defense outside), regardless of whether the fire or the blitz is being used. The remaining backs block to the outside of the cup, and protect the inside seam also (Diagram 11-13).

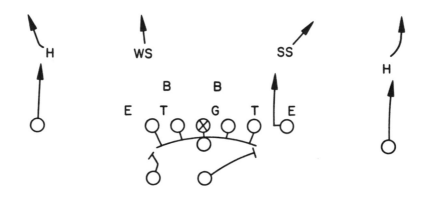

DIAGRAM 11-13

THE PLAY OF THE DROP-BACK PASS

As can be seen, the drop-back passing attack can be very complex or can be made very easy. Three, four, and five man pass patterns can be employed and these patterns are dependent upon the defensive coverages, alignments, depth and width of the pass routes and cuts, what the offense desires to accomplish, etc. In many cases, the offensive team can send out one or two receivers to one side or the other and use maximum protection for the quarterback. Diagram 11-14 illustrates a drop-back passing pattern to the split end side with the many reads and keys, rules and techniques explained. In numerous cases, the ball will never get to the split end, because of the coverage in the defensive secondary. The quarterback can pass to the tight end or flanker if the defensive coverage deems necessary. This is just one example of the multitude of pass routes and patterns that can be utilized by the offensive team and the slight adjustments necessary before and after the snap of the football.

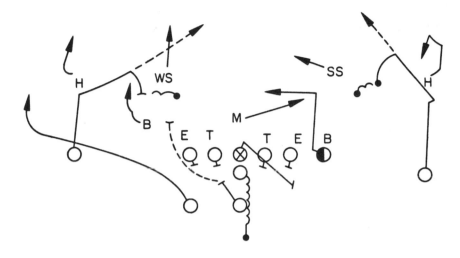

DIAGRAM 11-14

OFFENSIVE LINE

Tight End

Release inside (4 deep) and key the mike linebacker. If he does not stunt or vacate, run an eight to ten yard route and drag for an open area. Key any linebacker (such as mike) in your area.

Interior Linemen

Utilize man on man principles with the offensive backs. Since flow has been called to the left by the quarterback, block right if uncovered. Be aggressive, stay low, head up, wide base, bulled neck, and recoil or ride according to the defensive man's rush. Keep the feet moving in short, choppy steps.

Split End

Take a good split from the offensive tackle. Release from the line attempting to get a head up relationship on the defensive halfback. Read the movements of the weak side safety for coverage. If he comes forward automatically, run a post route and look for the ball quickly. If the weak side safety retreats, run the required curl pattern and key the outside linebackers movements. Slide according to coverage.

OFFENSIVE BACKFIELD

Flanker Back

Release from the line of scrimmage and obtain a head up relationship with the defensive halfback. Key the movements of the strongside safety. If the strongside safety should come up, run a post route (do not run into the middle). If he should retreat, stay with the curl pattern.

Tailback

Release from the backfield and key the defensive halfback. If he retreats, stay close to the line of scrimmage. If he should come up, then get deeper into the secondary. Once near the sideline turn up field and look for the ball immediately.

Fullback

Since flow is called to the left key the mike linebacker. If he comes, block him. If not, look to the outside. If no rush occurs, then release outside to a vacant area. You are a safety valve.

Quarterback

On the snap of the football, the quarterback keys the mike linebacker. If he should come or vacate, hit the hot receiver immediately. If the mike man does not, then the quarterback reads the strongside safety. If this man comes up, the quarterback should hit the flanker immediately on the post pattern. A quick touchdown is better than a ten or twelve yard gain on a curl pattern. If the strongside safety reverts to the deep middle, the quarterback should stay with the percentages and throw to the flanker side. If the strongside safety does another maneuver, the quarterback will look directly to the split end and attempt to hit him on either the curl or post cut. If covered, the quarterback scans to the tailback route. The quarterback can hit the tight end dragging across if open also.

Other Pass Patterns

There are a multitude of patterns that can be utilized versus entirely all pass defensive secondaries. However, some routes and cuts are better and gain more success versus certain coverages. Once the coach knows the secondary coverages of the defensive team, he can better install the patterns necessary for success. The following patterns (Diagrams 11-15 through 11-19) are a few examples that can be executed with and/or without reading and keying of the defensive secondary and linebackers. It is the coach who decides whether the quarterback will read and go with the percentage passing game or whether he will take his chances with primary and secondary receivers. Both have their advantages and disadvantages.

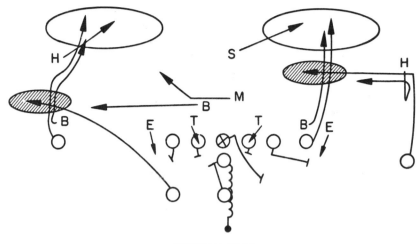

DIAGRAM 11-15

Good versus 2 deep zone and man to man underneath. This can be read by quarterback and receivers with the pass route being adjusted.

The flanker, split end, and tight end read the outside linebacker for coverage versus the 3 deep diamond secondary.

DIAGRAM 11-16

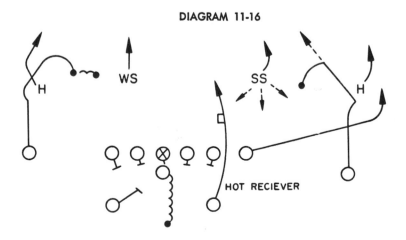

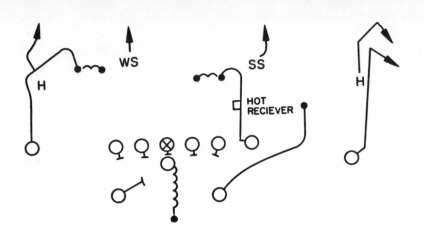

DIAGRAM 11-17

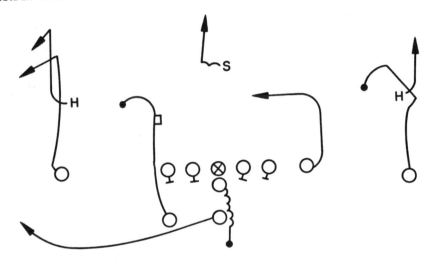

DIAGRAM 11-18

DIAGRAM 11-19

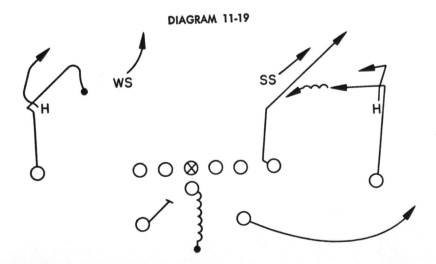

The Quick Passing Game

One of the finest pass attacks from the drop-back pass which can be utilized at any time is the quick pass. Quick pass plays are illustrated in Diagram 11-20. When the defensive team does not cover in the short flat areas, the offense should attack them as quickly and as feasibly as possible. The split end and flanker will run approximately 5-yard quick routes. They will either execute the hitch, out, glance, or slant pass. The patterns will be dependent on how the defense covers the flanker and split end. The tight end will release from the line and read the mike linebacker. If the linebacker stunts or vacates the tight end is the safety valve. He will be hit automatically by the quarterback. If the linebacker does not come, the tight end will continue upfield as illustrated. The protection can be executed in two different ways. The linemen can either fire-out and strike the opponent across the line of scrimmage, or the line can quickly set up in a pass protection cup and block the defensive line. The quarterback will read the secondary coverage before the snap of the football. He will pass the ball to the most open receiver. The quarterback will take two quick steps backward and key the mike linebacker. If he should fire or vacate, the quarterback will hit the tight end with a pass. The tight end, of course, can yell "hot" "hot" if necessary. If the mike does not come, the quarterback will pass the ball to either the split end or flanker which ever one is open.

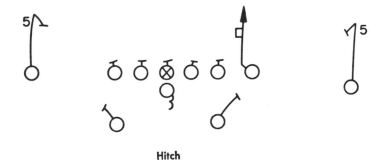

Hitch

DIAGRAM 11-20

Out

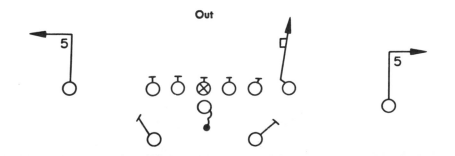

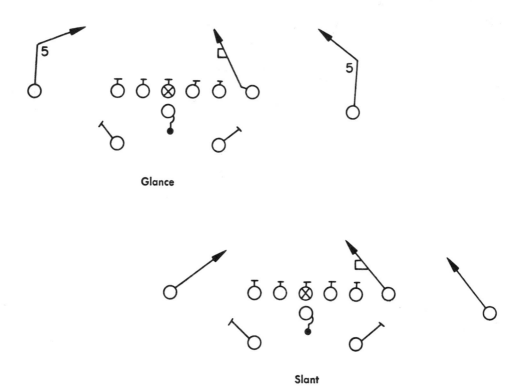

Glance

Slant

Special Passes

There are numerous passes which can be utilized from the dropback pass series that can be considered special, because it attempts to "trick" or outmaneuver the defensive opponent. These can be delayed passes or any other type of play. Diagrams 11-21 and 11-22 illustrate, as examples, two special plays from the drop-back sequence of plays.

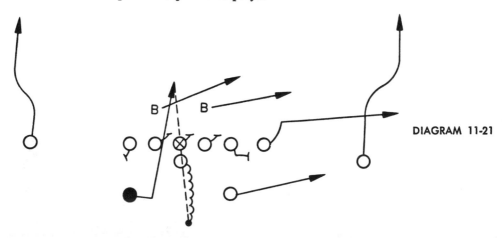

DIAGRAM 11-21

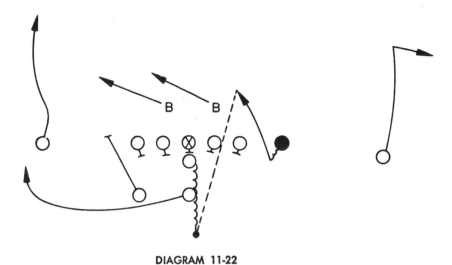

DIAGRAM 11-22

Draws, Screens, and Shuffle Passes

If the offensive team is experiencing a great deal of pressure because of the defensive team's rush, the offense can easily employ draws, screens and shuffle passes. A fullback draw is indicated in Diagrams 11-23A and 11-23B. The tight end releases and blocks the strongside safety man. The interior linemen ride their men the way they go. The onside guard and center, however, can cross or boom block versus a few defenses. The split end and flanker drives the defenders deep and peel back inside. The tailback sets for a pass and releases for the linebacker on his side. The fullback sets for a pass also, and is handed the ball by the quarterback. The fullback runs over the right guard and keys the blocking in the area. He runs for daylight. A quarterback draw is indicated in Diagram 11-24.

DIAGRAM 11-23A

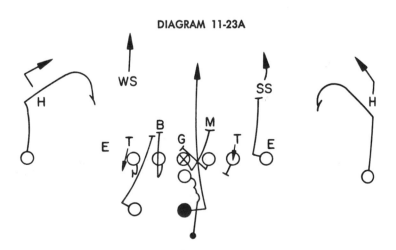

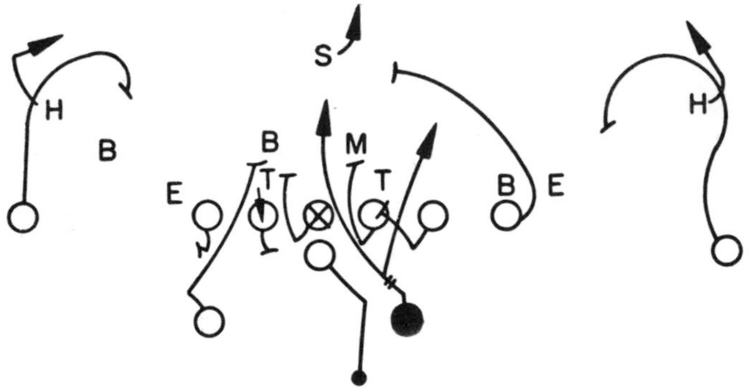

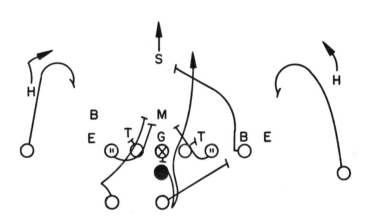

DIAGRAM 11-23B

DIAGRAM 11-24

An excellent maneuver versus a rush is the check series to a hot receiver from the draw play. Since it is difficult to run a draw with a rush (especially inside) a check to a tight end or halfback can be implemented. The quarterback takes the ball from center. As he retreats for the draw and sees any type of rush, the quarterback pulls up and hits his hot receiver who is keying the mike linebacker also. The quarterback will stop short as the fullback sets, raise up and pass to one of the check receivers. Diagram 11-25 illustrates a check series pass from the draw **play.**

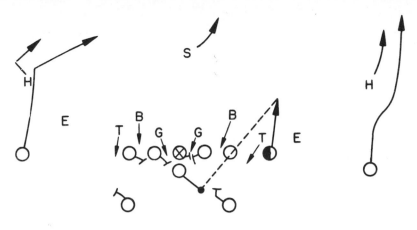

DIAGRAM 11-25

The screen is excellent against the rush of the defensive front alignment. There are numerous types and styles of screen passes. The coach can employ screen passes to ends or backs and can utilize the screen to the left, middle, or right. A double screen can also be employed. A screen pass to the left is shown in Diagram 11-26. The left tight end will drive the defenders to his side deep. When the screen is thrown, he will turn back and block one of the defenders. The left tackle, left guard, and center will pass-protect for three counts. It is important for these men to strike their opponent two or three times before going to the screen area. The left tackle will sprint-out toward the sideline and block anyone coming from the outside. If no man comes, he will turn upfield. The guard will block anyone to the inside. The center will sprint out and turn upfield for any defensive ball players. The left halfback will fake a block and release to the screen area to receive the football. The right guard and tackle will continue to protect the passer's backside. The right end and flanker will release from the line of scrimmage, go across the field and attempt to get in front of the play. If the screen is to the right, the same techniques are executed (Diagram 11-27). A double screen is shown in Diagram 11-28 versus blitzing linebackers.

DIAGRAM 11-26

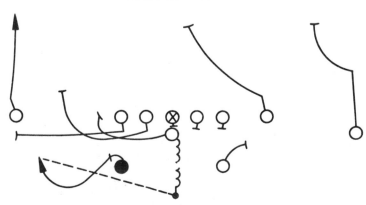

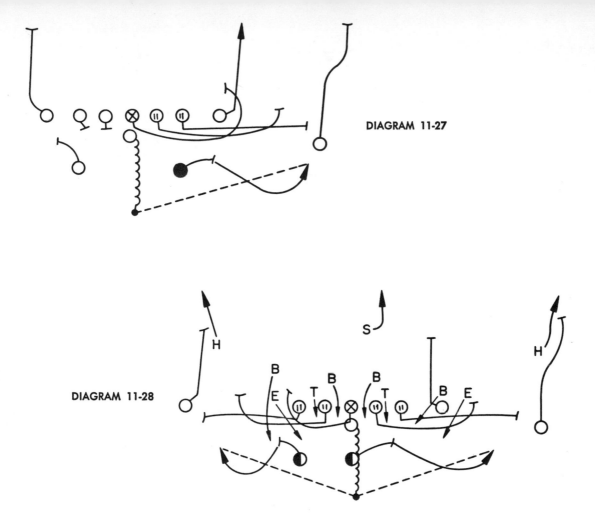

DIAGRAM 11-27

DIAGRAM 11-28

Shuffle passes to the offensive halfbacks are good also when the defensive team is employing pressure on the quarterback. Diagram 11-29 indicates the quarterback retreating and shoveling the football underhand to the tailback. The offensive linemen can employ cross, trap, and boom type blocking according to the defensive set, maneuvers, etc.

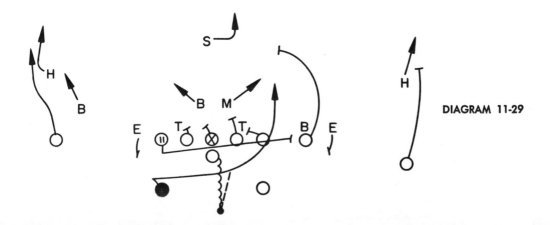

DIAGRAM 11-29

Index